Mindful Parenting

ALSO BY SCOTT ROGERS

Child Is the Cosmos
Mindful-Parenting Meditations
(Compact Disc)

Mindful Parenting

Meditations, Verses, and Visualizations for a More Joyful Life

Scott Rogers

Drawings by Jorge Perez-Rubio

MINDFUL LIVING PRESS
2005

 Printed in the United States of America. For information, contact Mindful Living Press, 4045 Sheridan Avenue, No. 196, Miami Beach, Florida 33140.

Cover art: *Mother and Child,* stone carving by John Tiktak

Cover photograph and author photograph by Kat Silverglate

Library of Congress Control Number: 2005934001

ISBN: 0-9773455-0-5

For information about special discounts for bulk purchases, send inquiries to: contact@mindfullivingpress.com.

First Printing, December 2005

10 9 8 7 6 5 4 3

for Pam

for everything that you are, and

for giving life to Millie and Rose

You are the bows from which your children as living arrows are sent forth.

The archer sees the mark upon the path of the infinite, and He bends you with His might that His arrows may go swift and far.

Let your bending in the archer's hand be for gladness;

For even as He loves the arrow that flies, so He loves also the bow that is stable.

—Kahlil Gibran, *The Prophet*

Contents

Acknowledgments *xi*
Foreword *xv*

Part I Connection: The Joy of Mindful Parenting

Opening to the Present Moment 3
Why Practice Mindful Parenting 6
Developing a Mindful-Parenting Practice 14
Mindful Parenting and Verses 23
Mindful Parenting and Meditation 29
Getting Started 34

Part II Verses: Mindful Moments

Opening to a New Day 43
Opening to Recurring Pleasures 73
Untying Life's Knots 93
Opening to the Unexpected and to Sadness 103

Part III Meditations: Journeys to Awakening

Meditation Exercises 115
Self-Guided Journeys 141
Visualizations 147

Closing 175

Appendices
Appendix A: Twelve-Step Mind-Body Flow Exercise 179
Appendix B: Breathing Exercise 183
Appendix C: Mindful-Parenting Children's Story 185

Acknowledgments

My life is delicately sandwiched in between my two wonderful parents, Susan and Arvey Rogers, and my two loving children, Millie and Rose. Whereas the substance of a sandwich generally resides in its center, in my case it is found on the outside, with my parents and daughters. I could not have written this book without the lifetime of support and love I continue to receive from my parents. The many joys found in the nooks and crannies of mindful parenting would be lost to me were it not for the lessons my daughters teach me every day and the love they share in every moment. I am always grateful for the gift of their presence in my life.

I owe a great debt to the teachers I have had the good fortune to meet and learn from over the years. Much of my personal journey has been nourished alongside the coast of Big Sur at a special place called Esalen. The workshop leaders I have spent time with and learned from include: Anna Wise, who taught me that there was a method to the magic of an awakened mind; Gregory Kramer, who shared his wise lessons on how to bring mindfulness meditation into everyday conversation. This insight, which continues to flower in my awareness, surely is responsible for my bringing together mindfulness and parenting. I also wish to thank Dennis Lewis, whose exercises and lessons in breathing helped bring me into a deeper place of calm and presence; Sharon Salzberg, whose thoughtful listening and wise words manifested when I needed them most; and Krishna Das, who shared his love and devotion to Neem Karoli Baba with such honesty and ease that it spontaneously deepened my capacity to be present in the here and now.

Because meditation forms the bedrock of this book, I bow with gratitude and respect to the members of the Miami Beach Sangha and the Naples Community of Mindfulness, whose collective presence strengthens my practice every day of my life. It would be difficult to measure the impact of Marty Peters, who, in 1991, introduced me to formal sitting practice, but I suspect that she first watered the seeds that blossomed into my interest in group meditation. I am deeply grateful to Rabbi Mitchell Chefitz, who, in 1976, infused me with knowledge that there was a deep spirituality residing within us all, and then seventeen years later, while preparing for my wedding ceremony, shared the importance of loving-kindness and the power of meditation.

Although I have never met Thich Nhat Hanh, we once shared the same path as he led a walking meditation in a park in Oakland, California. Because of his insight and the ease and love with which he shares the miracle of mindfulness, I smile every time I wake up. I would not have started this project were it not for his book, *Present Moment, Wonderful Moment: Mindfulness Verses for Daily Living*. His student, Fred Eppsteiner, has become my teacher. I was unaware how important a teacher is to one's spiritual growth until the moment I first heard Fred speak during a Day of Mindfulness retreat, and it instantly became clear.

This book is but a stepping-stone—for myself, and for those who may find its content meaningful. It remains a work in progress, and where its language and purpose falter, I am solely responsible. I am indebted to those wonderful friends and family members who took the time to read and comment on an early draft: Leila Fisher, Arvey Rogers, Susan Rogers, Stacey Edelman, Jill Siler, Neil Stollman, and Steven Trattner, and to Bill Blatt, for posing questions that caused me to rethink and better articulate the concepts underlying mindful-parenting practice. Thank you, David Kramer and Laura Rywell, for not only reviewing the manuscript but for meeting with me to discuss the nuances, and to offer guidance and insight. Thank you, Diana Burnett, Melanie Camp, Sheri Cholodofsky, Joan Davidson, Andrea England, Mark Metz, Nicole Metz, Regina Rogers, Shana Rogers, and Meryl Wolfson for your support of my efforts to explore mindful parenting and to share it with others. I am especially grateful to Jeffrey Gordon for the many hours we spent exploring mindful parenting, and for being there the moment the idea for this book manifested.

Where the book speaks easily and resonates deeply, I owe much to Marshall Fisher and Lilly Golden, for taking the time out of their busy lives as parents and writers to seriously review and edit the manuscript. Melissa Hayes, thank you for painstakingly editing the final draft, and, with your husband, John, helping me to develop a more satisfying book.

Foreword

Following the birth of my second daughter, I ran across *Present Moment, Wonderful Moment: Mindfulness Verses for Daily Living*, by Thich Nhat Hanh. It is a wonderful book that continues to shape my life. The book presents short verses, intended to be contemplated throughout the day, that serve as reminders of one's transient nature and connectedness to the Earth and the cosmos. I memorized several verses and would recite them at specific times during the day as a way to wake up from routine and take notice that I was alive and breathing, that my feet were touching the Earth. As a result, I began to slow down. Breaking away from whatever I was doing, even if for a moment, grounded me. When I returned to the task at hand, I did so with a fresher mind. Some of the clutter that had begun to build was cleared away. I found that the process of repeating these verses resulted in mindful moments arising with greater ease.

After having incorporated mindfulness verses into my daily life, I not only found that I had acquired a tool with which to awaken from an automatic, mindless state, but I also began to feel more connected to the world around me. Moments of connectedness became associated with feelings of joyfulness.

Being "present in the moment," however, took on a special significance when I was with my children. In addition to the calmness and serenity that would flow through me as I became more mindful, I felt a deeper sense of well-being and happiness. To further explore these feelings, I created mindfulness verses applicable to parenting. To my delight, I began to find that the most routine moments with my children, even those that generally might be associated with stress and anxiety, became infused with joy. I then wondered whether I could experience such happiness when I was away from my children by bringing them into my awareness. I found that I could. It is no surprise that people fill their work spaces with pictures of their children and loved ones.

The feelings that emerged were not new. I felt as if I were reliving, even if for a few seconds, those extraordinary moments forever emblazoned in my soul: witnessing the birth of my child and holding her for the first time; cutting the umbilical cord, knowing that this beautiful child was leaving the safety and comfort of her mother's womb and moving into our care; watching my newborn fall asleep in my arms and snuggle asleep in her crib, nurse at her mother's breast, take her first steps, and, when she got older, run to me when I returned home in the evening, arms opened wide, smiling broadly, and shouting *Daddy!* as I lifted her into the air. For those of us who are not birth parents, the range of early experience and depth of feeling can be just as intense.

Moments such as these, though fleeting, resonated deep inside of me. They resonate deep within us all. So inspired, I began to develop mindfulness verses for every sort of parenting experience so as to connect more deeply with my children. As I began to incorporate these verses into my daily life, parenting became immensely more fluid, and many routine experiences became profound. I was tapping into a deep source of joyful energy and bliss that had always been within me, silently waiting for me to take notice. And now, with the aid of mindfulness verses, I was doing so. This was no panacea for my concerns with the world's woes, or even those that creep into my small space. Challenging times surely lie ahead. But the slow and steady, increasing awareness of what really matters in this world makes each day qualitatively more meaningful.

I have meditated for many years and, on occasion, have experienced spontaneous moments of bliss. Such times are rare and fleeting. But I believe that our deeply rooted connection to our children can serve as a powerful source of happiness, and verses are a convenient way to tap into this connection, as they can be recited anytime and call for but a few moments of attention. Indeed, verses are a short form of meditation.

Shortly after completing an early version of this book that contained only verses, I let the manuscript sit for a year, hopeful that missing pieces would reveal themselves. During that time, I developed a website, www.themindfulparent.org. In it, I placed samples of the verses. Early response to the website was positive, as parents from around the world wrote in expressing their interest in becoming more present and better grounded in their interactions with their children. Importantly, parents were seeking both smoother interactions with their children and a deeper sense of calm and presence in their lives.

An offshoot of these communications was the development of mindful-parenting visualizations—meditations utilizing visual and sensory imagery that incorporate both the physical and spiritual presence of one's child. Due to the widespread interest in these meditations, I developed the mindful-parenting meditation CD, *Child Is the Cosmos*, which was sent to parents and child-care givers throughout the United States and in over eight countries. As it became clear that the parent-child connection could help foster greater mindful awareness through the recitation of verses and visualizations, it made sense that this connection could also aid in the development of a meditation practice. At that moment, things clicked. Just as the verses and visualizations had evolved, I began to explore how traditional meditation techniques might be modified to incorporate awareness of one's child into the meditative process. A variety of techniques emerged, offering parents and child-care givers an additional avenue to explore in their efforts to start meditating, or to help them maintain their meditation practice. Put together, the practice of mindful parenting emerged in a more mature form, offering not only verses, but also many different methods of deepening spiritual awareness and becoming more present.

The second section of this book contains mindful-parenting verses applicable to many different moments we experience throughout the day, and during the course of our lives. Each verse is followed by a commentary on its relevance to our relationship with our child. The third section contains mindful-parenting meditations. This section includes meditation exercises and guided visualizations that can be used to begin or enhance a more formal sitting meditation practice. So as not to favor one gender or a particular family size, the verses and visualizations alternate the use of female and male pronouns, as well as the singular and plural. I hope that parents of children of all ages find the verses, meditations, and visualizations to be useful tools to help them tap into deep, flowing currents of joy.

The following section presents an overview of the nature and practice of mindful parenting. For many, this will be an important stepping-stone to using verses and meditations and developing a general appreciation for the practice; for others, preliminary material of this kind distracts from the process. For those who prefer to dive right in, feel free to skip the introductory section that follows and begin with the verses and meditations. If you can comfortably incorporate one or more of the verses or meditations into your daily life, take it as a sign that you have missed nothing. If instead you are one who prefers to examine the road map prior to departure, the next section will serve as a succinct guide. Of course, whichever path you take, no road is ever foreclosed. Like parenting—and life itself—the opportunity for greater learning, fulfillment, and joy continually presents itself anew.

Scott Rogers
Miami Beach, Florida
June 5, 2005

Part I

Connection

The Joy of Mindful Parenting

Opening to the Present Moment

We live in a fast-paced world with a never-ending supply of distractions to absorb our time and attention. We wake up in the morning and, before we know it, we are out the door. We move from one task to another until the day draws to an end. At the end of the day, feeling exhausted and stressed, we find comfortable distractions to tide us over until we fall asleep. And then we repeat the process all over again. It's like the instructions found on a shampoo bottle: *Wash. Rinse. Repeat.* Only instead, it is *Rush. Distract. Repeat.* For those of us who have spent our entire adult lives in this type of world, it is all we know. Slowing down can be an unfamiliar experience, and even unsettling. We don't know what to do with ourselves, and we desperately seek out the nearest distraction, be it television, the Internet, movies, food, driving, or reading. All of these serve important purposes, but can be abused if we turn to them to avoid awakening to what is really going on.

To truly *be* with our children requires that we slow down. We have to discard our chronic tendencies to focus on the future and dwell on the past, as they have no place in the moment, and only distract us from being present with our children. The good news is that we all seem to share the desire to slow down. We sense the importance of being able to sit still and do nothing. But despite our will to slow down, we remain unable to stop ourselves from maintaining a frenetic momentum. As a result, we may feel guilt or frustration, and finally resolve that we simply are powerless to do anything about it. Thich Nhat Hanh refers to "mindfulness" as "keeping one's consciousness alive to the present reality." When we do so, we acquire the insight to make decisions deliberately and to live our lives more in accordance with our truest wishes for ourselves.

Were our lives simpler and were we confronted with fewer distractions, we would be more aware of our children's presence in our lives. As a result, we might feel, more deeply, the raw emotions that emanate from within the bond we share with our children. Instead, it is far more likely that at any given moment of the day we are not thinking of our children, not even aware of their existence in this world and of their presence in our lives. And on those occasions when we do think of them, often it is because we feel anxious about some event or circumstance; we are concerned with where they are and whether they are safe. As a result, the joy implicit in our connection to our child is overwhelmed by the distraction of the moment. Mindful parenting helps to reorient ourselves to our connection with our children. As a result, we experience the extraordinary feelings that accompany such awareness. Importantly, we do not need to alter the main activities of our lives. We simply insert into what we are doing the space of mindfulness. The moment still passes—work gets done—but we introduce an element of awareness that, over time, enhances the grace and joy life has to offer.

It is wonderful to feel fully the deep connection that exists between us and our children. We feel an intense love when we wrap our arms around our children and they wrap theirs around us. We share a deep embrace and time stands still. The future and the past are beyond our comprehension. We are living in the here and now. But when exactly does that joyful feeling fade? When we release the embrace? When our child leaves our presence? When we lose sight of her? When our thoughts turn to someone or something else? The answer is that the feeling survives as long as our heart and mind remain aware of our child's existence.

To be mindful of your child is to feel her presence, wherever she may be. At times your child may be miles away. Is it "out of sight, out of mind" until you see her again? At other times your child is inches from you. Have you taken this for granted and forgotten she is there until something awakens you to her presence? And when your thoughts turn to your child, whether she is holding your hand or across the globe, do you allow that moment to penetrate your being so that the connection between you and your child, and ultimately, all of us and the cosmos, is energized, or do you treat it as an everyday event, barely noticed? If it is the latter, then you have cut yourself off from a flow of energy and aliveness that presents itself, truly beckons to you, every moment of your life.

At birth, the umbilical cord is severed so that your child may mature into an autonomous being capable of surviving on her own. Not surprisingly, we consider ourselves separate and distinct from our children. But the depth of closeness and connection that exists at birth between parent and child fades only at an intellectual level. The heart of this duality is never compromised. This organic connection is a deep and powerful one that exists in full measure at every moment of our lives. It knows no barriers. But the physical, emotional, intellectual, and spiritual forms of separation that pervade our cultures and societies diminish our sense of this connection. To become mindful of the moment means to become aware of what is taking place around us and to become at one with the deeply rooted connections that bind us all together. This is one of the most direct means to feeling deep joy; compassion then arises naturally. Mindful parenting serves this purpose, immediately enhancing your connection to your child, and unlocking your connection to the cosmos. But merely recognizing that the connection exists is not enough. You must also open your heart so that you may tap into the ever-present connection, for it is then that resplendent joy emerges.

Why Practice Mindful Parenting?

We cannot expect to simply turn our attention to our children and immediately feel overwhelming joy. Of course, there are times when we do feel such joy, but life is too hectic and our relationships too complex for it to be that simple. More often than not, we feel too busy to turn our attention fully to our children, even for a moment. Doing so requires that we turn our attention away from something else, and we don't know how to do that. Among other reasons, we don't feel we have the "time." But, if we learn how to tune in to our children throughout the day, even if only for flickers of an instant at a time, we begin to accustom ourselves to the ease of doing so. Our ability to connect to our children deepens, and the naturalness of doing so becomes manifest. This expanded awareness wakes us to the present moment.

Initially, you will feel a mellow bliss. It is mild at first, but noticeable. With practice, the feeling becomes more definitive, more readily observable. And over time, a feeling of deep happiness will blossom. Most startling, you will learn to summon the joy present in every moment. This feeling transcends the moment, and you will find the space you need to feel comfortable letting go of yourself, and mindfully connecting to your children with greater ease—perhaps even effortlessly. You will naturally begin to open your heart, and you will do your body and mind good by repeatedly introducing into your life a state of joy. In doing so, you counter the chronic tension and stress that already pervades our lives and over time can wreak havoc on our health and well-being.

Because our connection to our children is so deeply rooted in our psyches, parenting is a particularly apt source of mindful expression. For example, if you were asked to describe yourself at a work-related meeting, you might state your occupation; describing yourself as a parent may not roll off the tip of your tongue. At the same time, if you were at a school function, it is likely you would identify yourself as a parent. The context very much defines our self-identification. But an important difference exists between our identity as a parent and that of businesswoman or artist or computer programmer. The former, at its core, is indelible, while the latter is transient. Parenting is a state of being that applies to every moment of our lives—whether we are aware of it or not.

The Power of Connecting with Your Child

As parents, we know the deep connection we feel toward our children. This connection is often greatest, and comes easiest, when our children are young and have not yet begun to establish their identities. How can you forget the first time you cradled your child in your arms, smelled your infant's breath, and locked eyes with your newborn; or the depth of emotion you felt when placing your sleeping child in her crib, silently watching her yawn, stretch, and dream? The feeling is one that transcends words; it runs as deep as our primordial soul.

As the child grows older and the tug and tussle of the process of identity development make everyday interactions more complex, feelings of connectedness become compromised. Without a mechanism to retain the openness of mind that breathes joy into our hearts, the rigmarole of our daily lives transforms the once-omnipresent feeling of deep connection to our child into one that arises only from time to time. Of course, intellectually we know that the love we feel is always there. But wouldn't it be wonderful to live that feeling every moment of our lives? The practice of mindful parenting enables the expansion of that feeling into every crevice of our daily life. By engaging in the various exercises of mindful parenting, the connection, like a ripple in a pond, grows to the point where it envelops us. Each of us has the capability to reawaken to these extraordinary emotions.

Because our lives can be so demanding, the struggle to succeed so deeply rooted, and the drain on our focused attention so severe, it is no wonder we perceive ourselves as separate from those around us. That feeling of separateness, however, is an illusion, an artifact established and maintained by a vigilant ego. Observe the deep bond between a nursing mother and her child. Or consider the pain you feel when your child is hurt. At these times, the lines suggesting our separateness blur. Were you a flower growing in a garden, your children would be the flowers growing alongside you. You would always be together, always breathing in harmony; you would move together with the wind, feel the sprinkle or pounding of raindrops against your faces, leaves, and stems.

You would intrinsically share the joy of survival and the threat of extinction. Life and death would ebb and flow. At no time would your children not be with you. At no time would you not be aware of your children. Of course, we are not flowers growing in a garden (or are we?), and our lives don't allow us to remain physically interconnected in the same close space. But the feeling of connection that mindfulness facilitates is a feeling that knows no physical boundaries and is not limited by space and time. Mindful parenting transforms the feeling of separateness inherent in our physical realities into one of closeness. And out of that closeness blooms joy.

At the end of our lives we will not be fretting over the money we didn't make, or be feeling elated over the fortune that we amassed. We will not be second-guessing decisions over which we once labored, or recalling some delicious meal we once savored. At the time of our passing, we will be recalling the people we loved and whose presence brought us joy. If we are fortunate, our children will be with us. Together, we will marvel over the wonderful time we shared together on this Earth. At that moment, we will be fully engaged in mindful parenting. Our hearts will open wide and receive a flow of love and joy that always existed, but had only been tapped into from time to time. But why wait until the end of life, when we can feel this way every moment of our lives?

One morning, as part of my meditative practice, I visualized myself going through various stages of my life. The visualization begins in the present and ends with myself as dust scattered in the wind. Midway through the meditation, I visualized myself on my deathbed surrounded by my children. Sometimes the meditative mind will breathe life into these images, and suddenly, I felt as if I were actually hugging and kissing my daughters, with a mixture of joy and tears. I lay there frail and peaceful as I looked to my two daughters, who had become grown women. As I was experiencing an intense outpouring of emotion, a simple thought came to my mind: "If only I could have another chance. As wonderful as this life was, oh, the opportunities I missed . . . the times I deliberately, foolishly turned my attention away from my daughters and focused on something that had no real meaning. What I wouldn't give to live those moments again!"

At that moment, unbeknown to me, my three-year-old daughter Rose, who had awakened from her bed and walked into the room where I was meditating, sat down cross-legged and, as I opened my eyes, smiled, and said, "Daddy, I love you." In a split second, I journeyed from old age to the present. Had I been given a second chance, or was I awakened to the value of living each moment fully?

Is there really a difference?

Mindful Parenting Is Not About Raising Your Child

You will not find any instruction in this book on how to deal with the challenging situations that arise as you rear your child. This is because mindful parenting is not about learning how to raise your child. Instead, mindful parenting is about you. When Ram Dass was asked how parents can best teach their children to become more spacious and interact with the world from a state of awareness, he responded, "You work on yourself to be a spacious, resonant environment that is around the child so that if the child chooses to come out and play, there is nothing in you that is going to keep them stuck." Life is filled with matters and circumstances that can overwhelm you, and it is necessary, for your own well-being, to find the tools and develop the skills to navigate comfortably through life's labyrinth. Mindful-parenting practice provides you with some of these important tools and skills. So equipped, you naturally become a better parent.

It is ironic that our children, perhaps the greatest source of joy we will know, can become involved in situations to which we often respond in anger, frustration, and anxiety. If we react automatically and mindlessly to these situations, they inevitably prove to be a source of great dissatisfaction, and we do a disservice to ourselves and our children. When this happens, we sabotage a precious opportunity to connect more deeply with our children—to be present for them in their state of need, and to be present for ourselves.

No matter how much care you may take to avoid those situations that provoke mindless reactivity, you cannot eliminate them from your life. But you can, through the practice of mindful parenting, reorient yourself so that you respond from a place of mindfulness. When this happens, the moment is transformed. And because your connection with your children remains strong, your manner of dealing with challenging situations becomes comfortable and fluid, your response more constructive. The magic of the moment becomes evident to you and your children, and great lessons are readily absorbed. Your children, as they instinctively begin to model your behavior, learn how to respond constructively to trying situations. As a result, the practice of mindful parenting helps you to become a more loving and compassionate parent—naturally. You will also find yourself better equipped to deal with both everyday challenges and the unexpected. The truly miraculous part of it all is that you will begin to draw insight and wisdom from a place of stillness deep inside of you that you did not previously know existed; or, if you did, were rarely able to access. You will become "the bow that is stable" that Gibran writes of in the epigraph to this book.

It is important to remember that mindful parenting is not about obsessing over your child. While the verses and meditations contained in this book all involve bringing your child into your awareness, it is not intended that everything you do that is meditative or mindful involve your child. To the contrary; mindfulness is actually an awareness of the present moment that need not be directed to your child's presence. In fact, meditation is, in its purest sense, an experience of emptiness and no-thought. But, as is discussed more completely in the remainder of this section and in Part III, your spiritual and physical connection to your child can help bring about meditative states of mindfulness and expanded awareness. This said, the spiritual ties between you and your child, when explored through mindfulness and without too much "thought," offer the opportunity for deep meditative experiences.

Mindful Parenting and the Passage of Time

We have all heard parents comment on how fast time passed as they watched their children grow. "It was only yesterday that he took his first step." "Can you believe she has her own apartment and is going to college?" Rarely, if ever, do we hear: "My goodness, her childhood passed at just the right pace. I vividly recall each and every exciting moment."

One reason why time seems to pass so quickly is that we are not aware of the moment as it happens. When we open to the present moment—reining in our racing thoughts and moving awareness into the body—our perception of the passage of time aligns with reality. When our minds are racing with thoughts of past and future events, both real and imagined, we miss the moment—perhaps entirely. Is it any surprise, then, that when we do recollect the fragments of that experience, the feeling is not satisfying?

One beautiful and quite tangible aspect of mindful-parenting practice is that time appears to slow down. In truth, you become more in tune with the passage of time. As a result, time passes at a comfortable pace. Just as important, you become more patient as you accept the natural flow of experience and allow time to do its thing. One powerful example is a mindful-parenting exercise that can be done every time you wash your hands. It may surprise you to learn just how many times in your life you have washed your hands. If you wash your hands six times a day, then you do so approximately two thousand times a year. While a single hand-washing may last only about fifteen seconds, over the course of years, the cumulative time spent washing your hands amounts to days and days. Ask yourself how many minutes, or even seconds, you can recall of the many days you have spent washing your hands. If you are like most people, the answer is probably very few. You may recall the time you cut yourself and had to wash very carefully around your injured finger, or when you first adorned a finger with a beautiful ring and stared at it lovingly, or worried about it slipping down the drain. But these sensational moments are few and far between;

most of the time is forever lost, if ever truly lived in the first place.

Instead of washing your hands in the same rote fashion as you have done practically all your life, breathe aliveness into the moment by singing or humming "Happy Birthday" to your child. Sense or bring to mind an image of your child at that moment, wherever he or she may be. Begin singing as you lather your hands and then proceed to wash them slowly and joyfully. Feel your fingers touching your palms. Smell the soap. Feel the wetness of the water. Smile when you hear your child's name. With mindful awareness of the presence of your child in your life, you not only slow down time but you expand your connection to your child. In this way, the moment is transformed from a nonevent into a joyful experience; it becomes one you will remember, perhaps for your entire life. You will actually begin to cherish the time you spend washing your hands. This exercise is but one demonstration of how the practice of mindful parenting can infuse everyday experiences with moments of joy, deepening your connection to your child.

Developing a Mindful-Parenting Practice

There is nothing easier than becoming more mindful. After all, it is the state of awareness we first experience as newborns, long before the rigidity of a complex society begins to mold us. It's as simple to bring about as taking a deep breath and uttering the words "I am reading." Go ahead—take a deep breath and say, "I am reading." Consider fully what those words mean at this moment. Doing so should have shifted your focus from the substance of this book to the fact that you are participating in the "act of reading." While nothing is easier than becoming mindful, few things are more difficult than sustaining mindfulness. Your attention probably has already shifted back to the substance of this book and away from the state of awareness that you are engaged in the act of reading. Did it?

So, how do you sustain a mindful practice? Simply put, with patience and practice. Mindful living, especially as it relates to our children, develops much like our bodies when we exercise. If you expect to become fully mindful overnight, you will be disappointed. You may be discouraged to the point of giving up. It is the same for people who join a gym in the hope of losing weight or gaining muscle strength, and find the process too slow. But those among us who stick with it, who make the time and are patient with the results, know that the slightest change can be a powerful thing to observe, a rich reward in itself. In time, we become more mindful, and the focus shifts to sustaining and enjoying the fruits of our practice.

Not surprisingly, the practice of mindful parenting infuses the body with joy and a sense of purpose that follows you throughout your day. It opens your heart and enables your sense of compassion to be expressed in ways that might otherwise have remained dormant. And this, in turn, inspires you to act with greater love and compassion, not just toward your children but to all those around you. You will come to realize that you are participating in a wonderful circle of experience as you are catapulted through space and time, a human being forever capable of greater personal growth and love.

Mindful Parenting and Mindful Living

If you have practiced mindfulness, you are probably accustomed to reining in your attention, focusing on your breath, and becoming acutely aware of what you are doing at the moment. A classic example is washing dishes. A person can wash dishes to get them clean, and a person can wash dishes simply to wash dishes. The person whose goal is to have clean dishes may be thinking about a million different things while washing them. He could be planning a vacation, anxiously pondering an undesirable future encounter, or even recollecting a mealtime conversation. While he may be washing the dishes, he is not with the dishes he is washing; he is not being mindful. In contrast, a person washing the dishes to wash the dishes is aware of the dish in his hand, aware of the feel of the sudsy water as he maneuvers the sponge across a dirty surface. He hears the squeak of the dish as he rubs his palm across it. He really hears the squeak—like a volcano erupting, like a crow cawing in a cornfield. His thoughts are not on the moment past or the moment future. He is truly washing the dishes. As a result, he is truly alive at that moment.

Unlike dishes that we hold in our hand, our children's physical proximity to us can be remote. Nonetheless, the approach taken in this book does not require that you be in close physical proximity to your child in order to practice mindful parenting. What is required is that you bring your child's presence into your awareness. The premise underlying mindful-parenting practice is that your connection with your children can be used to stimulate mindful awareness.

It bears noting that from one perspective, it may not seem that all of the verses in this book elicit the present moment.

For example, while driving a car, it may seem more mindful to be thinking "I am driving a car," rather than having, as one verse provides, brake-light colors cue images of your child's heart. Directing your attention to a child who is far away may seem like focusing on something that is not present at the moment. But, as is discussed below, because your child is present on this Earth (or in your heart), when you summon her into your awareness, you are attending to the present moment. Indeed, even when you mindfully wash the dishes, you tend to exclude from your awareness many things taking place right in front of you: the shape and color of the faucet and sink basin, the sounds around you, the view out a nearby window, and on and on. As the depth of your mindful awareness grows, you are able to increase the number and types of items you bring into your field of awareness.

Because the scope of our moment-to-moment awareness is limited, we have difficulty maintaining awareness of our child. This is the case even though they remain at all times a vital part of our life, and a vital life force in the cosmos. Were we truly mindful, at all times, we would know where we were in the universe and be aware of our body position. We would be conscious of our breath and how we felt; we would perceive the weather and the temperature, the moons, planets, stars, and galaxies. We would see not just the computer, movie, or television screen, or book page, or sandwich, or person—or whatever may be directly in front of us—but register, and keep in awareness, all the sensory stimuli around us. We would be aware of the people in our family, workplace, community, nation, and the world. We would be aware of animals, plants, trees, oceans, clouds, and the Earth's rich soil and dry sand.

We would be aware of the presence of disease and death, as well as birth and vibrant health and energy among all creatures of the world. We would be aware of the tragedies taking place all around us, as well as each and every miracle. In short, we would be aware of it all. We would sense and feel everything.

But, of course, we don't do this, or even believe that it is possible. We focus on what we believe matters most by eliminating all other distractions. By unconsciously eliminating so much, we cut ourselves off from that which grounds us. Mindfulness practice often begins by bringing into consciousness the fundamentals of our existence: our breath, and an appreciation and awareness for what we are doing and feeling in the moment. The object of our mindful state can begin and end with the breath. It can also expand outward to incorporate all of existence—to resonate with the rhythm of the cosmos.

But which of the myriad things taking place at any given moment do you choose to become objects of your awareness? One approach is to direct your awareness to those things that connect you most deeply to the cosmos. And while bringing anything that is taking place into your awareness helps further this connection—awareness of the leaf floating to the ground and the dirty napkin blown by the wind; awareness of your child running carefree in the playground, and of a soldier running from an explosion; awareness of the planet Mars and of a rock amid a heap of construction rubble—your human nature makes it easier for some things to register more deeply than other things. Generally, you will have an easier time summoning into awareness, and sustaining in awareness, those things closest to you. Doing so opens connections to the cosmos that, over time, have been closed or narrowed due to the blinders we all wear as we go about our daily lives. The tools and exercises for the practice of mindful parenting contained in this book are premised on the natural closeness and corresponding deep connection between ourselves and our children.

Wherever You Go, There's Your Child

You may be familiar with the extraordinary books and mindfulness teachings of Jon Kabat-Zinn. One of his books, *Wherever You Go, There You Are: Mindfulness Meditation in Everyday Life*, teaches that the source of our happiness and all the richness life has to offer is found within us. The title poignantly reminds us that we cannot escape ourselves, and that no matter what life has in store for us, whether good or bad, we will be there for it. If we appreciate what this means, then we are more likely to receive each moment as an opportunity to slow down the internal chatter of our mind and awaken to the fullness of the moment.

But who are "You?" If you go to sleep or fall unconscious, does the cosmos evaporate? Do wars cease because you stop thinking about them? Do rivers stop flowing when you watch television? Does your child disappear when someone cuts you off while you are driving? Of course not. But your awareness of the cosmos, war, a flowing river, and your child is very much influenced by the preoccupations of your mind and heart. Whether you realize it at the time or not, wherever you go, all of these things follow. You are connected to everything and everything is connected to you. The irony is that wherever you go, you find yourself—because there's really nowhere to go. It's your mind that moves about, while "you" pretty much stay put. And so, anywhere you go, your child is there with you.

The verses and meditations in this book cue us to the presence of our children in our lives. Most of us feel especially close to our children, or have, at one time or another, felt a deep connection to them. Whether we are physically present with our children or our children are across the world, we are *with* them. For this reason, the organization and presentation of the verses and meditations in this book do not distinguish between when we are physically present with our children and when we are not. But there is a difference worth discussing.

When we are mindful, we see what is before us. When we are not mindful, we see what is in our mind. I can vividly recall a time I was preparing dinner for my children. My daughters have never been big eaters, and I knew it would be a challenge to get them to eat anything. Hopeful, I had placed some broccoli on a plate in front of them and immediately began looking in the refrigerator for something else they might eat. "Aha," I thought, as I saw some macaroni and cheese, already prepared. While it was not the healthiest choice, at least I knew they would eat it. I recall taking the dish out of the refrigerator, turning automatically to my daughters at their little table, and saying, "Here, why don't you have this?" They both looked up at me, happily eating the broccoli. Of course, I had seen none of that. In fact, I had seen the opposite. So, even though my children were physically present with me at that moment, they might just as well have been miles away.

At other times, our children may be miles away, yet we are deeply in touch with them. We all know the feeling of being away from our children while our thoughts continue to turn to them. Perhaps it was while awaiting a laboratory or school test result, or maybe because the last time we had been together, they were fretting over something or were upset. Separate and apart from our shared concern over some future event, our minds and hearts were focused deeply on our children. We visualized them. We felt their pain. We connected to the heart of who they are and profoundly felt their presence.

I remember a moment when I became especially aware of the power of mindful parenting, and simultaneously, of its elusiveness. One morning, during meditation, I was feeling especially good. The morning was quiet and my practice felt effortless. My mind didn't wander much and I was attentive to my breathing. Then my daughter Rose pushed open the door and walked in. "Ah," I thought to myself. "I will use this interruption as a reminder to become even more awake, to become even more mindful." I was feeling very satisfied.

What must have been a few minutes later, I realized that Rose was jabbering away about something. I, of course, was focusing on my breathing and not letting my thoughts stray; I had stopped paying attention to what was happening. Then, I looked at her, and for the first time actually heard what she was saying. She was crawling on her knees, acting like a cat, repeating over and over again the phrase, "Meow . . . Wake up! Meow . . . Wake up!" There before me was my beautiful daughter, with a broad smile. Love poured out of my heart, and I reached over to pull her close and embrace her, releasing my meditation posture. Where had I been prior to that moment? There is a saying that you can't see the tree in front of you until you see the one behind you. Merely because you are physically present with your child does not mean that you are mindful of her. Similarly, you can be physically quite distant from your child and nonetheless be truly *with* her.

This experience reminds me of one recorded by Peter Matthiessen in his book, *Nine-Headed Dragon River: Zen Journals*, where he relates an experience he had rising from a prolonged sitting meditation:

> When I finally stand, no wiser than before, the pain unravels with such violence that, during walking meditation, my teeth are chattering. Even lying down in rest period my knees hurt. Then I open this notebook to set down my folly, and my child's photograph drops onto the bed—just . . . Alex! Nothing in the world but . . . ALEX! It is as if dark glasses had been snapped away. So startled am I that I burst out with a great laugh. . . . Silly idiot, cracking his knees off for a glimpse of "truth" and here is truth smiling at him from his own bed! ("Not knowing how near the truth is, we seek it far away.")

While we can summon our children at any time regardless of where they may be, the fact remains that it is easier to be mindful of our children when we are physically close to them. After all, they are right in front of us, where they serve as a cue to their presence, especially when their behavior is unusually good or bad. So, for example, if you are reading a bedtime story and become lost in the routine, your child's persistent call to *Show me the picture!* can remind you that you are alive, that you are blessed to be with and reading to your child, and can serve as a reminder for you to take a breath and become mindful of your breathing—all of which might otherwise have been lost in the shuffle to finish reading the story and get your child to bed.

But when you are not in close physical proximity to your child, unless you are anxious about some future event with consequences for him, you may be less likely to naturally turn your thoughts to him. Equally important, if something does cue you to your child's presence, it can be difficult to maintain this awareness. Such occasions may present the greatest opportunities for the practice of mindful parenting to infuse you with a sense of joy. In his fascinating work on "nonlocality," physicist Russell Targ finds in quantum physics a theoretical basis for concluding that everything that is, is available to your consciousness in every moment. This would, of course, include your child. It is precisely because you are remote from your child that engaging in mindful parenting can bring about the greatest transformation because doing so involves tapping into this deeper consciousness. It is at these times that we have the most to gain.

Mindful Parenting and Verses

While mindfulness can be practiced in many ways, this book utilizes everyday events to trigger the recitation of specially crafted verses to engage in mindful parenting. The verses serve two primary purposes: (1) expanding and enriching your connection to your child; and (2) bringing you into the present moment. Reciting a verse in the manner described below opens your awareness to the presence of your child, enriches your sense of connection, and brings you into a state of calm.

Consider the verse, "Walking":

With every step I take, my child's heart beats

The verse orients your attention toward your child, calling on you to sense your child with each footstep you take. This awareness is grounded in the physical and organic presence of your child in the world. In addition, the verse elicits a sensory experience. When you recite "Walking," you not only shine awareness on your child, but you sense your child's heartbeat. You might imagine your child's heartbeat both by visualizing it and by hearing its rhythmic pulse. Other verses may elicit a variety of other sensory experiences. This is a deliberate and important part of the process: A fuller experience is possible when the verse engages a rich network of sensations and connections within the mind and body. We all differ in our ability to bring objects to mind that we can then visualize, touch, smell, taste, or hear; be sure to draw on the forms of sensory experience that work best for you. Finally, the verses directly or indirectly remind you to breathe deeply as you recite them. The process of breathing deeply, integral to your ability to slow down and move into a state of calm, forms the cornerstone of practically every meditation, relaxation, and mindfulness practice. The physiological benefits of deep breathing are now well accepted.

While it may be very pleasing to rest awareness on your child, and doing so may spark your deep spiritual connection and trigger enjoyable feeling states, waking up to the present moment is a qualitatively different experience. Opening awareness to your child's body, however, *serves as a cue to opening awareness to your own.* Once that link is made, and your awareness comes full circle, waking up is close at hand. Accordingly, this is the second purpose that the verses serve, and the more important one in terms of moving into a state of mindfulness. As noted above, most of the verses draw attention to a physical aspect of your child's presence. Once your connection to your child is stimulated through reciting a verse, awareness of your child's body serves as a beacon that can redirect awareness to your own body.

In this way, awareness of your child's hand can bring awareness to your hand; your child's feet to your feet; your child's heartbeat to your heartbeat; your child's breathing to your breathing. And once awareness is brought home to your body, you can expand it to incorporate perception of movement, sounds, taste, touch, and smell. This in turn orients you more squarely into the here and now. You'll know this when it happens because your hands will look and feel different—somehow more alive and vibrant. Soap smells more fragrant, music sounds fresh and original, the sky bursts into view, and the taste of food lingers as you chew.

The following example may prove helpful. You are having a conversation with a colleague. You sense yourself becoming aggravated, and a verse comes to mind, momentarily opening awareness to your child. This awareness centers on your child breathing, and so, for a flicker of an instant, you become aware of your child's breathing. This feeling may be subtle. Then again, it may wallop you. Either way, you have expanded the scope of your awareness, poking a small hole in the state of aggravation. The next, and most important step, is then to use the image and awareness of your child's breathing to cue awareness of your own. Wow! You're breathing. How long has it been since you last realized this wonderful fact? As Robin Williams said, "Reality: what a concept." From this point you can expand awareness outward and deepen your connection to the present moment.

In an effort to make this process straightforward and easy to apply, Appendix A sets forth the *Twelve-Step Mind-Body Flow Exercise*. The exercise begins by having you place awareness on your head, working its way down to your feet. Sensing your feet, you more naturally can open awareness to the fact of your touching the living Earth, which then directs your attention to your breathing. From there, awareness flows to the top of your head. Your eyes open and you *see* with clarity of mind. Once you have experienced the full mind-body flow and memorized it, you can apply it every time you open awareness to any portion of your child's body. Then, when you become aware of your child's body, direct awareness to the same part of your own body and start the body-energy flow from that point. In the event that a verse does not orient you to a specific part of your child's body, or you simply open awareness to your child in general, direct your awareness to any portion of your child's body and then turn to your own. By following the mind-body flow, the process will become easier and the experience will grow richer.

The incorporation of meditation into one's life is a process that can take months, if not years. It is a lifelong endeavor. As the mind and body move farther along a spiritual path, states of well-being, joy, love, and compassion continue to deepen. But it is by no means necessary that one first develop a deep practice before these states arise. They arise spontaneously, during meditative moments. Each verse in this book offers you the opportunity to transform routine moments of your life into meditative moments. This is to say that when you recite a verse with intention, you are meditating. The recitation may take but a few seconds, but during that time, you enter into the heart of a meditative experience.

Reciting one or more verses on a regular basis unlocks your ability to enter into deeper and more prolonged meditative states. Each time you recite a verse, your "meditation muscle" flexes. The beauty of moving into the space of meditation and stillness is that every little movement is profound. Indeed, each of us has always meditated in one form or another, even if for only little bits of time here and there. For many, meditative moments arise during physical exercise, while engrossed in a game or sports activity, while crocheting, or when running into someone unexpectedly. But the process of establishing a meditative practice that has the capacity to transform us is a different matter. It starts with baby steps and few expectations. With intention and perseverance, our meditation muscle—our capacity for stilling the mind—develops. In time, a meditation practice becomes second nature. Eventually, it re-establishes itself as first nature. Throughout, we more naturally interact with those around us in a healthy, optimistic, and helpful way. And because we come to see the world from a place of presence—with a deeper understanding of the ebb and flow of life's offerings, and the impermanence of all that is—we move through life in harmony with everything around us, because we stop distinguishing ourselves so sharply from our environment.

The Use of Verses

If you find just one verse in this book that you incorporate into your daily routine, you will change your life in a wondrous way that will continue to unfold with the passage of time. In time, as recitation of the verse becomes spontaneous, you may want to add another verse. Be patient with yourself as your practice grows. One verse is enough for a lifetime. Also, feel comfortable taking liberties by modifying the verses presented. The only object is to engage in a process that can transform an automatic moment, in which we are living in forgetfulness, into a mindful one. With a little practice, these moments of awakening will prove self-reinforcing as they become increasingly easy to express, and more likely to be cued in moments to come.

Consider also drawing on your own personal experiences. Nothing is more powerful. Hopefully, the verses in this book will provide insight into how to transform a routine experience into one shining with mindful luster. A friend of mine shared a wonderful experience he had with his five-year-old daughter. The two of them spend a lot of fun-filled time together playing video action games on their television. They each have their own "joystick," which they manipulate cooperatively to advance some graphical hero through an adventure of increasing difficulty. As my friend described it, the two of them become extremely focused on the excitement of the game and the coordination needed to conquer each new hurdle. One time, when they had succeeded in mastering a new level of difficulty, my friend was ready to advance the game to the next level. At that moment, his daughter leaned forward, reached out her arms—her fingers spread wide apart—took a deep breath, and, smiling, said, "Take a moment!" So happy was she at that moment that she knew she wanted to savor it! This story beautifully illustrates how "Take a moment!" can become a powerful verse, and portions of a video game a wonderful mindful-parenting cue.

MINDFUL PARENTING AND MEDITATION

Every day, more and more people are looking to meditation to bring balance and a sense of calm into their lives. Many see their lives as stressful, and sometimes out of control. Whether a meditative practice takes root depends on one's ability to replace the habit of looking for and engaging in distraction with the habit of stilling the mind and returning to the present moment. As is explained in this section, mindful-parenting verses, meditations, and exercises can help you start, maintain, or expand a meditation practice in unique ways due to the powerful connection between parent and child.

All too often, painstaking efforts taken to learn and apply meditation techniques end up resulting in little, or unsatisfying, meditation. I often hear people express their frustration in not having "perfected" the art of meditation with statements such as "I just can't sit still for fifteen minutes," or "My mind is all over the place." But, as with many aspects of our personal growth and our sometimes compromised self-acceptance, we are too hard on ourselves. The reality is that it *is* difficult to start meditating. I have met few experienced meditators who do not readily acknowledge the challenges they continue to face in their practice. In fact, not only do serious practitioners share their challenges, but they also acknowledge that even the most stable of mind states is impermanent, and bound to ebb and flow.

One source of this ebbing is the mind's resistance to moving into a meditative space. Often, this is explained as the unwillingness to let go of control and to trust what unfolds. When we meditate, we try to stop latching on to the thoughts that run through our mind. Our thoughts cajole us into leaving the here and now and joining them on a roller-coaster ride of pleasure, pain, anxiety, enthusiasm, fear, and desire. If we're attentive, we recognize these thoughts as just that—thoughts. They come, they go. We watch the roller coaster, but we do not become the roller coaster. But, as is more often the case, in forgetfulness, we identify completely with the thoughts, and off we go. For the life span of each thought, we become, in turn, satisfied, pained, anxious, enthusiastic, fearful, and full of desire, as if that is all we are. We lose ourselves in our thoughts. We forget that we are so much more—that we are everything.

Despite the best of intentions, it is easier to want to "watch your thoughts," "watch your breathing," or "recite a verse or meditation" than to actually do so with regularity, intention, and awareness. But it becomes a little easier to do so when you incorporate your child into the meditative process. Because the practice of mindful parenting can open the doorway to a more fulfilling meditative practice, Part III contains several mindful-parenting meditations and meditation techniques that can guide you on the path of meditation, or help sustain your meditation practice.

It is worth noting why it is that awareness of your child can help exercise the meditation "muscle." A good example is found in the basic meditation technique of following the breath. With this practice, you sit still and focus attention on the breath. Commonly, this is done by counting each inhalation up to ten and then beginning again, or sensing the air flowing in and out of the nostrils. The sustained repetition of this practice, especially when done in deep concentration, can lead to wondrous states of expanded awareness, and perhaps even a dropping away of the thinking mind. The practice is ageless and powerful. One of the challenges, however, is to not give up. Another is to engage in the process mindfully, with the energy of the mind and body continually focused on—and when that focus falters, redirected to—the breath. The challenge is not the act itself, for the instruction is quite simple. The difficulty resides in learning how to avoid the distractions that persuade you to think about something seemingly much more interesting than the breath.

The culprit here is our sense of self—our ego. This wonderful entity has protected us from our earliest days. It simply would not know what to do with itself if it were to let go of controlling everything. Even worse, it is scared about what might happen were it to let go. As a result, it humors us in our spiritual quest only up to a point. The deeper we progress in our meditative practice, the more persistently it works to pull us out of it. It is only through perseverance, and the experience that follows, that we come to appreciate at the deepest of levels that these fears and concerns are fantasies and illusions.

Fortunately, even your ever-vigilant ego likes to think about your child. In fact, it finds your child so compelling that it can be lulled into a state of comfort and relax its vigilance when you direct your attention in this way. For this reason, the meditations and exercises contained in this book draw upon imagery and sensory experience of your child. As a result, fewer obstacles appear in the pathway of your meditation practice. You sit a little longer. You breathe a little deeper. And all the while, your meditation "muscle" gets stronger and stronger. Also, because your child is comprised of both a physical body and a spiritual body, the depth and expanse of connection that develops as a result of your increased awareness is that much richer. While your ego may be delighting in matters organic, a deeper aspect of your nature is touched by your growing awareness. Of course, it is not necessary that your child be integral to your meditation. And, if he is, it is not necessary that that remain the case forever. This is a personal, emotional, and spiritual decision. But for the reasons just mentioned, opening awareness in this way can be helpful.

In addition, many wonderful and popular meditation techniques and practices can be modified to incorporate your child. By doing so, you expand the possibilities inherent in these powerful meditations, and, because we all tend to grow bored (or are tricked by our egos into thinking we are bored), you can make alternatives readily available. One example is the loving-kindness meditation, designed to open your heart and expand your capacity for compassionate expression. While there are a variety of methods, most center around the wish for yourself and others to be safe, happy, healthy, and to live with ease. It was in Big Sur, at Esalen, that Sharon Salzberg introduced me to the specific language and structure of the loving-kindness meditation that is presented in this book. I've modified the last stanza to incorporate "ease of heart," as imparted to me by Krishna Das. This meditation involves wishing these states of well-being for ourselves, a benefactor, a friend, a neutral person, one who challenges us, and then, all beings. A mindful-parenting adjustment would be to add, or simply meditate on:

May my child and I be safe
May my child and I be happy
May my child and I be healthy
May my child and I live with ease of heart

Because this variation introduces one's child into awareness, there may be a more natural tendency to turn to this meditation intuitively. In addition to serving as its own meditation, you can turn to this beautiful loving-kindness verse anytime during the day, for no reason at all, or when your mind begins to jostle itself with disturbing or difficult thoughts and images. And, of course, if you have more than one child, you may substitute "children" for "child." The loving-kindness meditation exercise is presented in Part III.

As noted above, the beauty and beneficial nature of many timeless meditation practices may become more accessible when modified to incorporate your child. These, and the variety of other exercises contained in Part III, are designed to start the meditation ball rolling, or kick-start a practice that may feel as if it is floundering. You may find, as your meditation practice deepens, that your child plays less and less of a role. Just as your children naturally become less and less dependent upon you as they mature, so too, as your meditation practice matures, do you start to let go of their hands.

GETTING STARTED

The quality of your love and affection for your child is true and pure, regardless of how mindful you are. Still, the relationship you have with your child takes on a new dimension when you engage in mindful parenting. Mindful parenting enriches your heart by allowing you to tap into a connection between you and your child that runs through the core of your existence.

The next section of this book is comprised of a series of mindful-parenting verses. The verses cut a wide swath across parenting and the various situations you will encounter, both with and without your child. It is not intended that every verse be incorporated into your daily life. Certain verses will resonate within you more than others. As noted earlier, some of the verses are applicable when interacting with your child, while others come into play when you are physically separated from your child. Most of the verses are organized by the course of the day's events. You may want to modify some verses so that they are easier to remember or have greater meaning for you. The more meaningful verses will be those that touch you, bring about a sense of calm, and ground you in the present moment. You can also create your own verses to draw more intimately on your own experiences and moods.

Some of the verses draw on imagery that may make it difficult to apply them to more than one child at a time. For those of you with more than one child, you may want to focus your attention on the child that naturally enters your thoughts at the time. With many verses, more than one child can be brought to mind. For example, often I will utilize the "Walking" verse so that each footstep summons a different child's heartbeat. When the left foot touches the Earth, I sense Millie's heartbeat. When the right foot touches the Earth, I sense Rose's heartbeat. Also, because those of you with more than one child likely have a different relationship with each child, application of a mindful-parenting verse may be deliberate, so as to deepen your connection to a particular child at a specific time.

Mindful parenting can help alleviate some of the misgivings you may feel when separated from your child. Perhaps you are working, or on a vacation, and you feel guilty that you are not with your child, or you simply wish you were together. By expanding your awareness of your child's presence, you are in a very real sense connecting with your child; that is, you are embracing your child with your awareness. Often, feelings of guilt are learned reactions that reverberate only through your mind. By placing awareness on your child, and becoming more aware of the present moment, you draw energy from the mental chatter that feeds the guilt feelings. At the same time these feelings diminish, you naturally feel closer to your child.

The verses in this book are guides or signposts to help explore life more mindfully. Ultimately, the underlying experience associated with attending deeply to a mindful verse is our awakening to the bliss of the present moment. With practice, it arises spontaneously and with increasing frequency. Be sure to breathe deeply before and after reciting the verses. Because breathing is so integral to the practice of mindful parenting, Appendix B describes a basic breathing technique.

Following the collection of verses, you will find a section containing a series of meditations and meditation techniques.

These meditations can be incorporated into your daily sitting meditation, or, if you have been interested in establishing a daily meditation practice but have encountered difficulty in doing so, may help you take this first step. In addition to the formal meditations, visualizations and meditation exercises are included to offer you additional guidance and opportunities for incorporating more meditative moments and experiences in your daily life.

This is not a book to be read in a single sitting and then returned to a shelf. Nor is it necessary to explore the verses and meditations in the order presented. You may want to flip through the various sections to get a feel for the different scenarios to which the verses pertain. You may also wish to write down on a cue card a verse or two that resonate with you. Use these cards to remember the verses and to recite them at desired times. Place a verse by your alarm clock, in your car, beside your computer, inside your wallet, in your child's bedroom—wherever you would like to shine the light of mindful parenting.

After you find a verse you plan on using, sit with it in silence, mull it over in your mind, and rehearse it a few times. Speak the words and listen to your body. Be receptive to the thoughts that come into your mind. You might want to have this book with you, or scribble down the verse to read from as you recite it. Attend to the words as you slowly recite them, and take note of where you are and how you feel. In time, you will become cognizant of the shift in attention away from the rote and into the mindful.

Part II

Verses

Mindful Moments

Part II Verses: Mindful Moments

OPENING TO A NEW DAY

Morning Routine

Waking Up in the Morning 44
Going to the Bathroom 45
Brushing Your Child's Teeth 45
Drinking a Morning Beverage 46
Eating Breakfast 47

Leaving Home

Getting Ready for School 48
Walking into the Sunlight 49
Walking into the Snow 50
Walking into the Rain 51
Starting the Car 51

On the Road

Driving Your Child to School 52
Leaving Your Child at School 53
Traveling to the Office 54
Stopping at a Traffic Light 55
Watching Windshield Wipers in the Rain 56
Driving on the Freeway 57
Brake Lights 58

During The Day

Arriving at Work 59
Enjoying a Laugh with Colleagues and Friends 59
Sitting at the Computer 60

Composing an E-mail Message 61
Deleting an E-mail Message 61
Feeling Stressed During the Day 62
Feeling Hunger Pangs 62
Eating Lunch 63
Drinking Water 63
Making a Phone Call 64
Walking Out of the Workplace 64

Home Again

Traveling Home at the End of the Day 65
Walking into the Nighttime 65
Arriving at Home 66
Greeting Your Child 67
Preparing Dinner 67
Eating Dinner 68
Taking a Shower or Bath 69
Reading Bedtime Stories 69
Preparing for Bedtime 70
Watching Your Child Sleep 70
Relaxing at Night 71

OPENING TO RECURRING PLEASURES

Early Pleasures

Waking Up with Your Child 73
Taking a Nap with Your Child 74
Feeding Your Child Baby Food 74
Changing Your Child's Diaper 75

Everyday Pleasures

Playing a Game with Your Child	75
Speaking on the Phone with Your Child	76
While Your Child Is at Play	77
On the Computer with Your Child	77
Laughing with Your Child	77
Hugging Your Child	78
Writing a Letter	78
Reading a Book	79
Enjoying Time with Friends	80
Helping Your Child with Homework	80
Making Love	81

Nature and Exercise

Looking at a Sunrise or a Sunset	81
Experiencing Nature	82
Observing Trees	82
Looking at a Full Moon	83
Walking	84
Anytime	85
Exercising	85
Stretching	86

Important Moments

Birthday Party	87
First Day of School	87
When a Tooth Falls Out	88
While on Vacation	89
Looking at Your Child's Creative Work	90
Discussing Spirituality with Your Child	91

Untying Life's Knots

When in a Dispute with Another 95
Ending a Relationship with Someone Close 96
When Your Child Competes with the Television for Your Attention 97
When Your Child Is with a Babysitter 97
When Your Child Acts the Contrarian 98
When Your Child Cries 99
When Your Child Is Frustrated to Tears 100
When Your Child Challenges You 101
Being Interrupted by Your Child 101
When Disciplining Your Child 102

Opening to the Unexpected and to Sadness

A Child's Injury 104
Consoling Your Child 105
When Your Child Has a Fever 105
Feeling Depressed 106
Seeing an Accident on the Road 107
Feeling Sick 107
A Family Member's Passing 108

Opening to a New Day

Each morning we are presented with the wonderful opportunity to meet the day—and its challenges and pleasures—with an open mind. To do so, however, requires that we approach the day fully aware of ourselves and our connection to our surroundings. Otherwise, our actions will be guided by something other than the truth, and the outcomes we endeavor to bring about may have unintended and undesirable consequences.

Many of these challenges and pleasures are recurring events. It is as if each day, we have a renewed opportunity to work on those things that we have not yet mastered. We can use the cues of these repetitive events to engage in mindfulness. One of the greatest difficulties in becoming more mindful is acquiring the insight to break away from mindless actions. This is difficult precisely because most of the time we act mindlessly. How often does the day pass by so quickly that you can barely keep up with it? Before you know it, the day is over. Where did it go?

The following verses, which comprise the largest grouping of verses in this book, draw off of the seemingly mundane events of the day. Incorporating the verses, even just one or two, will radically change your perception of the day. These verses will help to slow your pace, and will permit you more time to process information, help you disentangle yourself from stress, and allow you to breathe deeply with greater frequency. At first, this may prove to be difficult. But a genuine effort to incorporate one or more of the verses into your daily life will lead to their being triggered with greater ease. And because the verses connect you to your child, the routine events of the day become infused with meaning. It's time to wake up!

Morning Routine

Waking Up in the Morning

My eyes open to a new day
My beautiful child
Slowly stirring in bed

The day can begin in a whirlwind, or it can begin from a point of calm. The difference is not dependent on what your morning entails, but rather on how you choose to attend to it. Each morning you awake to a new day and another opportunity to feel joy. Turn your thoughts to your child just prior to arising from bed. Breathe deeply before reciting the verse. And then breathe deeply again after reading it. There is such joy to be felt in the moment between and during breaths. Slow this moment down and visualize your child in her bed, awakening as you have just done. Stretch your body and imagine your child stretching. If you yawn, imagine your child yawning. If you rub your eyes, imagine your child rubbing hers. Let this synchronicity bring a smile to your face and allow you to enjoy this gift that life has given you.

Going to the Bathroom

My body is
My child's body

Because going to the bathroom is a regular occurrence, it can serve as a foundation for mindful parenting that, over time, can become very powerful. At every moment of the day and night, our bodies accumulate waste and prepare to eliminate it. This verse reminds us of this bond of the body that we share with our child. Use this time to visualize the inner workings of your child's body. It is a miracle that our bodies work as they do.

Brushing Your Child's Teeth

My teeth inside me
Will soon be clean and bright
And my smile
Will sparkle like the sun

Everyone feels differently about brushing their child's teeth. Some love every moment of it, and others find it very frustrating. Because it is a time we spend with our child, this verse, which my daughter Millie and I made up when we were together on a trip to Wyoming, can be shared with your child at the time of brushing. Recite it aloud and invite your child to join in. Brushing teeth may even become easier and more fun as you both become more mindful of the moment, and frustrations recede.

Soon enough, the process of brushing your child's teeth (and their own brushing) will become automatic. This verse reminds us that we are cleaning our teeth, making our bodies healthier, and opening ourselves up to the world with our beautiful smile. You may find that not only does this verse awaken you at this precious moment, but it may also inspire your child to enjoy brushing her teeth.

Drinking a Morning Beverage

As I bring this cup to my lips
I close my eyes
And inhale my child's out breath

As you take your first sip of coffee, tea, or juice in the morning, your child is probably nearby. Wherever he may be, he is breathing. And you are breathing. How often we forget! Start the day embracing your connection to your child, and your aliveness. He breathes out, you breathe in. Let the drink in your hands, and the first conscious breathing of the day, initiate this sensation. If the beverage is hot and steaming, sense the steam rising out of the cup as his exhalation.

As with many of the verses, this one asks you to form a mental image of a physical interaction involving you and your child. To enhance the power of the image, take a moment when you are with your child, and touch noses. As you look lovingly into your child's eyes, inhale as your child exhales. Be acutely aware of your actions and the sensations you are experiencing. Is his nose cold? How do you feel when his eyes lock onto yours? Are you both smiling? Can you feel the warmth of his breath as you inhale? The more mindful you are of this moment, the more intense your subsequent reflections will become.

Because we drink throughout the day, the time we spend sipping a beverage can serve as a wonderful cue to shift into a mindful-parenting mode. When verses, like this one, draw on repeated themes, or are themselves repeated throughout the day, their recitation can have a powerful cumulative effect. You may begin to feel a small tremor of fuzzy bliss at these times. Eventually, due to the mindful repetition of certain themes, you may find that as you shift into a mindful mode, a warm bliss will envelop you and bring about spontaneous joy.

Eating Breakfast

I am aware of this bite
And the grace of my child's life

We are fortunate to enjoy many meals with our children. But whether or not we are eating with our children, this verse serves as a powerful reminder of our child's presence in our life.

Breakfast marks the beginning of a busy day. Whether you wake up groggy or alert, by the time you sit down to eat, thoughts are beginning to churn in your head—much will happen in the next twenty-four hours. This verse contemplates awakening to the moment anytime during the meal. When you do, recite: "I am aware of this bite, and the grace of my child's life."

It is easy to take for granted the course of events that brought your child into your life. At any of numerous turns, it might have been different. Every moment is a blessing, and none should be taken lightly. So, too, we should not take for granted the ease with which we eat. Our mouth, tongue, jaw, and throat know just what to do. In fact, it is so easy—so automatic—that we can fly through a meal without ever taking note of what is happening around us, or inside us. How many meals have come and gone in forgetfulness? As you recite this verse, slow down your chewing and gaze at or visualize your child. Bring your awareness to your child's sweet smile. In the beginning, each time you recite the verse, you move from mindless eating into awareness. In time, you will find yourself observing this phenomenon as it happens, a sign that you are becoming increasingly mindful.

Leaving Home

Getting Ready for School

This ritual
Will not last forever
What color are my child's shoes?

Preparing for school in the morning can be a hectic time, as we ready our children and ourselves for the day ahead. Each morning will offer subtle variations. The days turn to years; before long, your child will finish school and move away from home. This verse, a reminder of the transient nature of this experience, may lead you to value it even more than you already do by seeing it for what it is—a beautiful moment to cherish. This verse is not intended to make you focus on the past with sentiment, or to concern yourself with a future that isn't yet here. Rather, it grounds you in the here and now; for right now, there is magic taking place around you, to which you need only open your eyes. What is the color of your child's shoes as he heads to school?

Walking into the Sunlight

Everywhere there is space
But when I touch the air
I touch my child

We owe our existence, and indeed, the existence of everything in our solar system, to the sun. On clear, sunny days, when the space between us and the many things around us appears empty, it is easy to forget that there is no emptiness at all, that there is no actual separation. What gives the impression of emptiness is, in fact, a space filled with billions and billions of molecules containing nitrogen, oxygen, argon, carbon dioxide, neon, methane, helium, krypton, hydrogen, and xenon. We constantly inhale these particles into our bodies; they are the same particles inhaled and exhaled by our ancestors, by all the world's inhabitants, and by our children on the day they were born and earlier this very day. We often forget about the billions of particles that fill this invisible space.

It's the same with our relationship with our children. Owing to our complex and sometimes hectic lives, our connection with our children can be choppy, and even feel empty, though at its deepest level that connection flows uninterrupted. We become so involved in our daily lives that we may not even be aware, from moment to moment, that our children exist. Our mind is elsewhere.

The next time you walk into the sun, recall that there is a thriving, energized, microcosmos between you and everything you see, and between you and everything you do not see. Look at your fingers. At the edge of your fingertips are particles that bump into and touch other particles, and so on, in a chain that reaches all the way to your child. Wave your hand and sense the ever so slight movement of air around your child, wherever she may be. Breathe deeply, and feel the gaps between you and your child slowly filling in.

Walking into the Snow

A snowflake
My child

Just as every snowflake that falls from the sky is unique, every child is unique. Snowflakes may float down leisurely from calm skies, and snowflakes may be tossed about in a snowstorm. In the course of your child's lifetime, she will experience all that nature presents. So as you watch the snowflakes fall, ponder the course of your child's life. From nature, and into nature, it is a frenzy of experience. If a snowflake lands on you, contemplate how your child's life is as durable and fragile as that snowflake's. In that moment when the flake's coldness touches you and melts into a drop of water, breathe deeply in the awareness that at this moment your child floats somewhere in the sky. Even if you are holding her hand, imagine her arms spread out from her body as she slowly floats to Earth from high in the sky.

Walking into the Rain

Rain cleanses the Earth
My child cleanses my soul

When it rains, water droplets from the sky clean our atmosphere. Rain may fall lightly as droplets bouncing against the pavement. It may also pound the Earth as clouds barrel across the sky. But no matter what form it takes, rain symbolizes cleansing and renewal. Your child's presence in your life serves the same purpose. Each moment of joy you experience as a result of your child's presence in your life opens your heart and cleanses your mind. Step into the rain and feel your child's presence as the water falls against the nape of your neck and across your shoulders and runs down your back, so that its pressure slowly eases away any tension you feel at the moment. Breathe deeply, and, as you relax your shoulders and un-hunch your back, smile with the thought that it is your child that eases you into this state.

Starting the Car

I put on my seat belt
And start the car
May my child be safe
As she steers her life

Every time we get into our car we embark on an adventure. Driving serves many purposes and has its associated risks. We buckle up and drive and seldom stop to think about what we are doing. Off we go. So it is with your child as he lives his life. You do what you can to ensure his safety, but ultimately, he is out there in this world, exposed. This verse reminds us that driving, like much of life, is all too often reduced to an automatic process. It serves to make us mindful of the vulnerable child out there in this wonderful and complex world.

ON THE ROAD

Driving Your Child to School

I see you in the mirror
How wonderful that we are together

The morning ritual of taking your child to school can be a rushed and hectic one, but this time of day actually presents a wonderful opportunity. This verse reminds us of how special it is to spend time together going to school. Soon you will drop your child off; you are together at this moment, laughing, or perhaps, crying. And sometimes your child sits quietly as you choose to listen to the radio or speak on the cell phone, barely aware they are even there. As you glance in the rearview mirror, you think you see your child, but you are not really looking at him. At other times, you may look directly at your child and not see him at all. When you truly see your child, you feel the awesomeness of the moment. This verse may be recited anytime you are driving with your child.

Leaving Your Child at School

Walking away from my child
I feel a tug
And I remember
We are connected

Perhaps one of the most interesting aspects of raising a child is the separation we experience, and how we deal with it. When our children start school, we find ourselves conflicted: We want our children to adapt comfortably to a new environment, and at the same time, we want them to remain close and to need us. At first, our children don't want to let go; but, in time, they adapt to their new environment. Sometimes they do so more quickly than we do!

The process is like that of a rocket ship pulling away from Earth's orbit. Sooner or later, it is time for the rocket to leave the Earth's orbit and head into outer space. At that moment, the rocket must overcome the Earth's tug. Our child, like the rocket, is directed toward outer space. We, on the other hand, may want to increase the gravitational pull and keep our child close. The verse reminds us that unlike the rocket ship which, when it leaves the Earth's atmosphere, may not return, we will always be connected to our child. The tug felt is an emotional one of attachment and fear of loss, and not one reflecting the true nature of our relationship with our child. In truth, there can be no loss, because we are always connected. This verse can be recited anytime we separate from our child.

Traveling to the Office

I am moving away from my child
But no matter where I go
My child remains with me

Some of us work outside of the home. Even if we work at home, we probably have carved out a secluded environment. Regardless of what form of transportation we take, or where our office is located, it is not uncommon for the day to pass with us rarely giving a thought to our child. Our lives can be very busy, and it makes sense that we would focus on our work. But being focused on solving a problem or getting a project done doesn't require that we drop awareness of our child. Our child is always with us. It is as if while we are en route to the office, our child is silently sitting on our shoulders or holding our hand. Were this the case, we would be pleasantly reminded of our child's presence in our lives throughout the day.

With mindful-parenting practice, you can maintain this awareness. And maintaining this awareness will add a sense of joy and quietude to what may be an otherwise complex and disruptive day. It may also facilitate your accomplishing work at a higher level of productivity and with greater insight. While you are traveling to work, take just a moment to imagine your child holding your hand. Direct awareness into your hands. Doing so, your finger tips will tingle as you relax your thinking mind and become more present.

It may not have been all that long ago that you were with your child. The gentle awakening can lend perspective when you find yourself overly frustrated, angered, or stressed by some issue at work, which you may already be struggling with in your mind.

Stopping at a Traffic Light

The traffic light is filled with color
I stop and take a breath
These are the colors my child is learning

We find ourselves in front of traffic lights and stop signs throughout the day. Rather than viewing these "stoppings" as an annoyance, you can allow them to create an opportunity to connect with your child, even though your child may be miles away. Green, yellow, red—the colors of the traffic light. You are stopped because the light is red. This can serve as a reminder, a mindfulness cue, to slow down inside. Take a deep breath and expand your belly. As you enter a state of greater calm, your attention turns toward your child who may still spend much of the day in a classroom. Recall the number charts, alphabet charts, and color charts that line classroom walls. Visualize your child sitting in school learning wonderful new facts. Whatever your child's age, learning never ceases, and whatever your child is doing while you are stopped, it surely presents an opportunity to learn and grow. As you recite this verse, visualize your child, sitting in a small chair in a classroom, excitedly learning the colors.

After sensing your child in a wonderful learning state, allow your eyes to gaze at the various colors surrounding you. For example, you may see a blue sky, white clouds, sunshine, green trees and shrubbery, the colors of the clothes you are wearing, and the colors of the cars alongside you. These colors are a miracle of the universe, and your eyesight. Again, these are the colors your child learns at school. When the light turns green and you accelerate through the intersection, be mindful of your child's ever-accelerating knowledge and wisdom. Pausing to reflect on the miracle of the learning process and the excitement it brings to your child is blissful. Every time I stop at a light, I feel a surge of spontaneous bliss.

Watching Windshield Wipers in the Rain

A beating heart
Wipes away tears
My child's heart
Is all I hear

When you drive through the rain and the windshield wipers are on, a wonderful confluence of events takes place. Whether they are tears of joy or tears of sorrow, the Earth is touching you. Just as you wipe away tears, the raindrops are wiped away with the pulsing of the windshield wiper. The blades' movement establishes a rhythm like the rhythm of a beating heart. At this time, allow yourself to hear your child's heart beating loudly, and consider the joys and sorrows life brings to you. For purposes of mindful parenting, it is not necessary to actually remember a happy or sad event (although that can be a powerful meditation). Simply appreciate that your child lives at this moment on this Earth, and that you can connect more deeply with his life force by identifying the rhythm in front of you with that of his beating heart.

Driving on the Freeway

I am a red blood cell
Breathing deeply as I
Flow through my child's body

I once had blood drawn, and then looked at the greatly magnified blood cells on a computer screen. Countless round cell bodies moved together, their denser centers filled with oxygen. Darting along the freeway, we can imagine ourselves in our car and those around us as blood cells flowing through our child's body. Our cars are the round red bodies that bring oxygen and life to our child. We notice other blood cells passing us by, also bringing energy to our child, and we notice blood cells coursing toward us within vessels traveling along a different route. Some are brand-new, and others are old. Some are powerful and others are sluggish. Visualize yourself on this wondrous journey, and connect with your child's body. Breathe deeply, infusing yourself with oxygen on your way to your child's heart.

This is also a wonderful time to explore the tremendous space above and surrounding you. The sky seems to go on forever. You may not realize just how much space there is within your body. We become so cramped, physically and emotionally, that we disconnect from much of the energy flowing around us. The visualization, "Meditation on the Vastness of Space in Small Places," found in Part III, explores your connection to your child in a way that expands awareness to embrace infinite space and time—space and time with which you can more fully connect with your child.

Brake Lights

Red lights
Blood cells

This verse builds on the verse, "Driving on the Freeway." How wonderful to take an experience as mundane, and sometimes annoying, as the appearance of brake lights, and turn it into a joyful cue. This simple verse can be used as often as brake lights appear. It reinforces the image of us as red blood cells in our child's body. Breathe deep and oxygenate! As with all verses, smile as you recite it. If it is nighttime, smile as you marvel over the flood of bright red lights filling the road before you. You may be surprised to find, when you see your child at the end of the day, just how much these simple recitations can enhance the joy of that moment.

The more sensory experience we bring into the moment, the greater the connection will be. If you have ever heard the swishing sound of blood flowing through the body, use this opportunity not only to imagine yourself as a blood cell coursing through your child's body, but also to allow yourself to sense the sound of that flow. Place the underside of your wrist close against your ear to hear this sound. If you become queasy at the thought of blood, this verse may not be for you. At the same time, the queasiness you feel, if not too uncomfortable, can serve as a powerful wake-up call.

During the Day

Arriving at Work

I have arrived
Where am I?

When you arrive at your place of work, you may find yourself in a state of mind that can become all-consuming. Take a few moments to contrast the feeling of "having arrived" with being lost. You may love your job, or you may be unhappy with it. You may have worked your entire life to be where you are now, or you may be stuck waiting for something better to come along. Regardless of whether your work fulfills you, it is likely you are physically separated from your children while at your workplace. This verse, contemplated as a parent, poses a question that is not easily answered.

Enjoying a Laugh with Colleagues and Friends

There is joy in this laughter
May my child and I
Always laugh together

The time we spend with colleagues and friends can be filled with laughter, humor, and wit. Such times are joyful and affirm the warmth and good feelings we share with other human beings. There is perhaps no greater joy than sharing laughter with our children. It is a doubling up of joy. When, during the day, you find yourself laughing, you can use this time as a cue to think about the laughter and fun you have with your child. Laughter flows from an open heart, and laughter opens hearts.

Sitting at the Computer

I connect with a mechanical brain
But there is a living brain
That loves me dearly

Our relationship with the computer has changed over time, as the computer has evolved from a glorified typewriter into an extraordinarily complex and powerful machine. And because we use it for myriad functions, including composing our thoughts, accomplishing work, communicating with family, friends, and business associates, and searching the Internet, the computer has become a large part of our lives. But while the computer is able to handle all these processes and functions because of its exceptionally sophisticated microchip brain, the computer does not love us. Most of us probably spend more time on the computer each day than with our children. During the day, when you become aware that you are on the computer (for example, when you experience a body ache or your computer screen freezes), you can recite this verse as a reminder of your increasing reliance on the computer, and that your child is not only far more brilliant than your computer, but possesses a heart and loves you deeply.

Composing an E-mail Message

Compose and send
Where is my heart?

Electronic mail is a wonderful thing. In the blink of an eye, we can communicate with someone across the world. Our e-mail communications may be personal or professional. In either case, we can lose ourselves in this seductive technology. Take a moment to reflect on the processes, both human and computer-involved, and ponder where your heart—your compassion—is at the moment you send a message. Is it with your child? Is it with anyone?

Deleting an E-mail Message

This message disappears
Like the hugs I give my child
Breathing in, I wonder
Is there a difference?

The act of deleting an e-mail message, not unlike throwing away something more tangible, is one that we often do in forgetfulness, especially if we repeat the act time and time again. The act's automatic, forgetful aspect becomes evident when we delete or throw away something important by accident. Better to be aware of what we are doing as we are doing it. The hugs and kisses we have given our children throughout their lives, like the e-mail messages we delete, can take place within an automatic state. The next time you delete an e-mail, recollect this verse and, breathing deeply, ponder the difference between a long since past hug and the message being deleted.

Feeling Stressed During the Day

This chest of mine aches
But not for my child

Consider those times of the day when you overreact to momentary stressors—or even react appropriately to extreme stressors. By shifting your attention toward your child, if even for a moment, you can assuage that feeling. Generally, when you find yourself overly anxious, you suffer because you do not feel you have sufficient time to do those things you need to do, or because you are concerned about some "possible" future event. As a result, your body reacts in ways that generate discomfort. This verse serves as a gentle reminder that your heart, if it should ache at all, should ache with love for your child. The momentary problem you are facing will, like most every problem, soon be a distant memory. And, as Michel de Montaigne once said, "My life has been full of terrible misfortunes, most of which never happened."

Feeling Hunger Pangs

My stomach is grumbling
The Earth nourishes my child

You may find yourself hungry during the day. Symptoms may include your stomach grumbling, as well as weakness and irritability. You respond to this feeling by eating. The food this Earth provides us is a miracle. It is sustenance that keeps us healthy, and we provide it to our children to keep them alive and well. Let your own hunger serve as a cue to the Earth's bounty and how it provides for your child.

Eating Lunch

As I swallow my food, I wonder
Has my child eaten yet?

Just as with eating breakfast, we can take this routine part of our day and transform it into something especially wonderful. At lunch, the swallowing of food can serve as a reminder of your child. He is going about his day and will satisfy his own hunger with a meal. Even eating lunch brings your child to mind; you can open up that moment in a way that might otherwise have remained dormant.

Drinking Water

Let me hug my child
With this next swallow

You may drink water throughout the day. Indeed, health professionals encourage everyone to do so. Each time you have a glass of water in your hand, let just one sip remind you to turn your thoughts to your child and embrace her with a hug. You may be surprised how much more awake you are the next time you embrace your child in your arms. It might just quench your thirst!

Making a Phone Call

I am calling someone I cannot see
I do not need to see my child
To feel her presence

The telephone is a wonderful device to bring us into contact with someone around the corner, or across the world, a person we cannot see or touch at the moment. This verse is intended for when you are away from your child, such as when you are at the office, traveling, or out during the day. The verse reminds you that there is much in this world that you cannot see or touch, but that is very much alive and present. One of these things is your child. You simply need to direct your attention to her in order to feel the strength and energy of her presence in your heart and in the cosmos.

Walking Out of the Workplace

The day is done
I follow my heart

At the end of a workday, you can take a moment to reflect on what you have accomplished. Perhaps you were productive and feel good about the day. Maybe it was a difficult afternoon and you are exhausted. No matter which it was, the day offered you countless opportunities to open to the present moment. Wondrously, it is never too late to do so. As you exit your workplace, breathe deeply as you begin your joyful journey to see your child. Listen to your body as your heart brings you home.

Home Again

Traveling Home at the End of the Day

The day is behind me
My thoughts turn to my child
Who may be thinking of me at this moment

When the day is done and you are on your way home, your thoughts might focus on the day's events and matters that still may be pressing. You can use the travel time instead as an opportunity to think of your family and mindfully open to your child. Take a deep breath. At that very moment your child is finishing up his own day, and soon you will be together. This is a nice opportunity to visualize your child. What is he doing? Is he thinking of you? Does he imagine that you are thinking of him? If you visualize this now, your reconnecting will be especially powerful.

Walking into the Nighttime

The darkness soothes
Missed opportunities
With my child

In the verse "Walking into the Sunlight," the sunlight alerts you to the particle world connecting you to your child. It awakens you to a connection you often forget about, and can arouse feelings of missed opportunities. When awareness shines on this connection, you see more clearly the gift of your child's presence. This insight, however, can lead to feelings of guilt or loss. But such feelings do not reside in the moment. They are triggered by reflections on the past and projected discomfort with the future. Instead, you can learn from the insight by accepting it for what it is. Nighttime provides this opportunity; it is a time for acceptance, regeneration, and healing. Let the darkness that flows over and around you act as a salve on these unsettled feelings, soothing you in the knowledge that you're doing your best and will continue to heal and grow.

Arriving at Home

I enter this sanctuary
With a fresh mind

Returning home after a long day's work, or after having gone out to run errands, is something that we do on a regular basis. How often do you park your car, get off a bus, or approach your home on foot and mindlessly unlock the door, enter, and turn to the television, or reach for the telephone or computer, without taking a moment to reflect on the wonderful fact that you have returned to the foundation of your family? This may be the place where you were born, where your child first lived after having been born into this world or brought into your family, where family celebrations take place, and where friends visit. It is the place where you have heard wonderful news, and perhaps the place where you have experienced heartbreak. Your home is the source of much of life's experiences.

When you walk into your home, you can do so fully aware of the sanctity of the place. You can sense the energy that has been poured into the home, which reverberates from within. As you touch the door, feel the metal or wood beneath your fingertips and against your palm. As you open the door and enter, perceive passage into a safe haven. Enter with a fresh mind. Try not to fall back on routine actions and reactions, but enter with a smile and an open heart.

Greeting Your Child

I return
To myself
One heart

While our ego creates a sense of separateness from our children, the fact is that our children are an expression of ourselves, and will survive us as our link to future generations. This paradox of separateness has many consequences to your developing relationship with your child. On the one hand, you can become too close, and on the other, too distant. Regardless of how you manage that relationship, at the deepest level you are one and the same. Embrace your child while reciting this verse and imagine the two of you as a single being. When your embrace ends, you may walk in different directions, but your heart and your child's will beat in time.

Preparing Dinner

This Earth and its beautiful colors
Feed my child

Whether we prepare dinner by cooking our food, by ordering take-out, or by having it prepared by another, the occasion offers us the opportunity to contemplate the nourishment we are about to receive. Eating is so much a part of our lives that we may take for granted the miracle of the Earth's bounty and its life-sustaining force. When we prepare to eat, we have the opportunity to interact mindfully with a substance that is very much alive. Enzymes, which are found in food before it is cooked, thrive, and the food's energy, which derives from the sun, is palpable. This verse invites you to take a moment while preparing a meal, or serving it, to consider the many colors and benefits of this wonderful gift from nature.

Eating Dinner

With every bite
My child and I
Walk hand in hand.

At dinnertime, we nourish our bodies with nutrition borne from the Earth. Regardless of whether you are with our child at this time, it is important not to let this moment speed by. Let the chewing motion awaken you to those times when you walk with your child, hand in hand, arm in arm. With each bite, you can imagine your arms swinging together, your hands interlocked. Sense the warmth of your child's hand and feel her fingers nestled in your grasp. If you are chewing too fast, slow down and savor this moment.

The verses for breakfast and dinner present two different images: your child's heartbeat (breakfast), and walking hand in hand (dinner). It is not necessary that you have a different verse for each meal. Consider the verses for breakfast and dinner, and, if you feel a preference for the sensory imagery of one verse, draw on it during any meal. If you choose to incorporate the same imagery at every meal, the repetition will allow the connection to build with increasing intensity.

Taking a Shower or Bath

As I wash this body
My thoughts
Are my child's thoughts

The depth of connectedness between yourself and your child runs deeper than any other you will ever know. When taking a shower or bath, you escape from all of the stimuli that you normally encounter during the day. You also find yourself alone in a very natural state. This moment presents a good opportunity to draw upon the core of the special connection you share with your child, who possesses, or has learned from, your flesh and blood, and your mind.

Reading Bedtime Stories

Turning this page
I take a breath
And marvel that I am here
With my beautiful child

Perhaps one of the most sacred moments we share with our children is when we read to them. At these times they are fully engaged. Are we? Take a breath as you turn each page and reflect on the extraordinary gift that life offers you at this moment. Smile with the knowledge that opening to this moment will slow it down and make it "real." No matter how mindful you become, you will finish the book and your child will fall asleep. But, if you take the opportunity to become more mindful, the reading itself becomes sacred.

In addition to being mindful while reading a bedtime story to your child, you may also read stories to your child that provoke imagery and ideas that relate to your inter-connection, and, when explored together, can expand that connection. An example of such a story, *One Day Winston the Wave Woke Up*, can be found in Appendix C.

Preparing for Bedtime

Night has arrived and we slow down
Thankful for the day
Tomorrow when we awaken
We will be together

As with the morning, the nighttime marks an important space in which to slow down and reflect: "Tomorrow when we awaken, we will be together." This verse is a wonderful one to share with your child. Take a moment and visualize waking up. Perhaps imagine yourself reciting the verse, "Waking Up in the Morning." How many nights and mornings have passed in a blur, forever forgotten?

Watching Your Child Sleep

Sweet child
Our souls embrace
In the stillness

There is something that touches us deeply when we watch our children sleep. Their breathing is rhythmic and deep. Their faces and bodies are relaxed. There is a stillness that envelops us. We can take this time to breathe deeply and relax. This is a wonderful time to soak in this feeling of calm. It is a feeling that we want to call to mind when we are with our children at more hectic times.

Whether you realize it or not, the calm sensation of stillness is always present. You simply need to be able to transcend the noise and chatter so that you can rest in the silence. When you leave your child's bedroom, reflect on the feeling in an effort to have it linger. Visualize your sleeping child and recite the verse again. Over time, you will develop a better handle on the feeling, so that you will be able to summon it when it's truly needed.

Relaxing at Night

The night sky is dark
Stars appear
Like my child's
Little surprises

We have all watched the night sky and marveled as twinkling stars slowly come into view. If you live in an area without a lot of city lights, the night sky may become saturated with stars. Even if you live where the city lights are bright, you will find some stars in the sky. The wonderful little surprises your child brings to you, the amazing things he says, and the wonderful way he makes sense of the world, are very much like twinkling stars, coming into view. And just like those stars, which are there every night, these miraculous moments never disappear. This verse reminds you of the natural wonder of your child's expression and growth. By reciting the verse, you can attune yourself to your child—the wonderful star that came out this very day—and marvel over him in the night sky of your mind.

Opening to Recurring Pleasures

There are events that take place throughout the course of our lives that can aptly be termed recurring pleasures. They are not the everyday events that are dealt with in the previous section. Rather, they are those wonderful moments that come about on a regular basis and constitute special occasions. Events such as these, by their very nature, encourage mindfulness. They are moments filled with love, enthusiasm, and, sometimes, anxiety. Mindful attention can ease the transitions to these times and accentuate the joy.

EARLY PLEASURES

Waking Up with Your Child

We awaken to the sun
A new day before us

This verse is one we can share with our children on those occasions we wake up together. Say it in the presence of your child, and one day she may join in with you. What a wonderful experience! It can also serve as a natural place to begin a discussion of what the day has in store for you—the things you are looking forward to, and those things that may cause trepidation. Most important, it provides an opportunity to share a part of yourself. If you take the time to open up and share what your day has in store, you include your child more deeply into your life.

Taking a Nap with Your Child

My child lies asleep in my arms
Awe and wonder

We often try to get our children to fall asleep so that when they do, we can rush around trying to get things done. If we allow ourselves to lie with them, study them, and focus deeply on who they are, we become more mindful of the precious gift we have been given. When your child falls asleep in your arms, you realize that you belong right where you are at that moment.

Feeding Your Child Baby Food

I feed you with a spoon
That is older than you

The miracle of your child's birth can sometimes be forgotten, especially when things are difficult. This can become the case when you first begin to feed your child, likely a new experience for both of you. All too quickly you can forget the extraordinary feelings of your child's birth and his presence in your life. This verse wakes you up to the reality of the gift of your child. Have you forgotten how recently he entered your life? And will you lose track of how quickly he becomes older than the spoon?

Changing Your Child's Diaper

The passage of time
Brings forth renewal and waste
Dependence and departure

When you change your baby's diaper, you connect at a very natural level. Your child depends on you. When you change a diaper, reflect on the transience of the moment with the knowledge that all too soon, your child will outgrow diapers. Before you know it, he will outgrow his clothes. Even as you toss away a diaper, your child is on his way to becoming an independent adult. This verse helps slow down your child's otherwise swifter-than-need-be development. Take a moment and feel the diaper in your hands.

EVERYDAY PLEASURES

Playing a Game with Your Child

When I was a child
Games were everything
Let me be a child again
By being my child

Our children love to play games, and they want to play games with us. But somewhere on the way to adulthood, many of us lose interest in playing children's games. If we do not share our child's enthusiasm, it can bring about feelings of anxiety and discomfort. And it does so at the very time we are together with an opportunity to connect.

If you play the game reluctantly, you may miss the beauty of your child's enthusiasm. Your child senses that you are detached, and this diminishes his joy. As a result, he doesn't lose himself in the game. But if you allow yourself to become immersed in the game with him, pledge not to allow your mind's ramblings to interfere, and pour yourself fully into this brief period of time, you will become one with him. This is no easy task. But as with all other aspects of mindful parenting, once the connection is hit upon, and the sensation of oneness flows, it becomes the easiest thing in the world.

Speaking on the Phone with Your Child

My child's voice
Emerges from the cosmos
Whom does she sound like?

When you speak to your child over the phone, you can experience the separateness and oneness of your relationship. If you listen deeply to what she is saying, her voice can flow through you. You smile as you imagine your child on the other end. If she is young, the experience can be very exciting for her. If your child is older, you can reflect on the many times you have spoken over the phone; of how once, when your child was younger, you spent a lot of time together. As your child speaks, sharing her thoughts and opinions, you appreciate that she is her own person. It's a miracle that your child is who she is. She came from deep within the cosmos. Can you hear the echo of her voice and trace its origin?

While Your Child Is at Play

Once we were inseparable
Now my child smiles in another direction

It is joyful to watch your child having fun. As she grows, there will be more occasions when she will find enjoyment in interacting with others. At times, you may get the sense that she has more fun with another than with you. This bittersweet sensation derives from a feeling of separateness. When the falseness of this feeling is appreciated, you will find that your child faces you from every direction.

On the Computer with Your Child

We marvel at technology
I now marvel at my child

It is easy to be impressed with the wonders of computers and technological advances. Innovations emerge daily. So it is with your child. All children have their special gifts to offer. When you observe your child interacting with the computer, take a moment to marvel over your amazing child.

Laughing with Your Child

My child's laughter is sunlight
That bathes my every cell

When your child laughs, you feel good. It is not just a happy feeling, but one that touches you deeply. This verse likens the laughter to sunlight. Just as sunlight bathes you with a flood of warmth, easing sore muscles, your child's laughter penetrates deep inside you. It brings a smile to your face and lifts your spirits, no matter how high they may already be.

Hugging Your Child

Our hugs will not last forever
But this moment is forever

Because the moment is all there is, we can perceive what transpires in a given moment as all there is. So, while your child's hug is transient, the moment is not. Just as you can count from one to two quickly, you can also spend forever approaching the number two if you cut the space between one and two into finer and finer increments. When you hug your child, fill the gap of the closeness you feel with no-thinking. Breathe deeply and time will begin to slow down. It will speed up again only after your thinking mind kicks into gear.

Writing a Letter

Writing this letter
I remember my child writing
For the first time

It has become increasingly rare that people write letters to one another. When we do, the act has the capacity to bring about a deeper state of presence. We write with deliberation. Mailing the letter involves an age-old ritual: licking the envelope, addressing and placing a stamp on it, and mailing it. In this fast-paced world, the idea that it might take more than a few seconds for a message to be communicated is becoming increasingly foreign. To many, writing a letter is a form of meditation. As you watch your hand methodically writing the words that comprise the sentences that comprise the paragraphs of your letter, visualize your child's hand and the moment he first scribbled the letters of the alphabet. If your child has not yet gotten to this stage, then think forward to what a wonderful occasion it will be when your child, hands so small, begins to communicate through the written word. Breathe deeply as you bring your awareness to your child's beautiful hand, and from it, to your own hand.

Reading a Book

My child's life is a story
Like the one told in this book
A book I will never finish

A poet was once commissioned by a rich merchant to write a poem honoring the merchant's family. The merchant's daughter had just given birth. After many months, the poet presented the merchant with the following:

Parent dies
Child dies
Grandchild dies

When the merchant complained, the poet explained that there was no greater blessing than to have a family's passing take place in the order presented in the poem. Indeed, this is how life plays itself out most of the time, though we are not always so blessed.

When we are reading a book, we immerse ourselves in another's story. Our child's life is its own story. It has a beginning, and we are somewhere in the middle. Awaken while reading a book. Grasp the book firmly in your hands and imagine that you are holding the book of your child's life. When you take a break from reading, put it down with care.

Enjoying Time with Friends

I sit across from my good friend
And visualize my child as an adult
Enjoying the same moment

It is enjoyable to be with good friends. We share experiences that bring us close and open us to great fulfillment. We may forget just how much our children are like us. They are beginning to develop social relationships. It is likely that they will develop friendships in much the same manner as we have. While enjoying a tender moment with a friend, imagine your child doing the same.

Helping Your Child with Homework

My child's mind is like the Earth
Every thought is a beautiful cloud
With each problem solved
Drops of rain dance on our skin

Homework can present a challenge to you and your child. You can become stressed if you feel pressured by time or have expectations for your child's performance. This verse invited you to appreciate the naturalness of your child's intelligence. Every thought that emerges is like a cloud passing overhead; it appears out of nowhere and slowly meanders. When a homework problem is solved, it's as if the clouds open up and release a delightful cool rain. Try not to focus so much on the answer itself. It is the miracle of being there with your child that bears noting.

Making Love

From this
My child's life
Life of my life

The act of lovemaking is full of emotion, energy, and pleasure. This verse, to be considered at any time before, during, or after the act of making love, brings to mind that this act brought your child into existence.

NATURE AND EXERCISE

Looking at a Sunrise or a Sunset

Another day
I have lived thousands
This moment together is precious
For it is all we have

Whether or not we are physically present with our child, the sunrise and sunset instill in us a deep sense of awe. Instinctively, we feel an inner calm. We journey around the sun every day and have been alive for tens of thousands of sunrises and sunsets. While looking at the sun's beautiful rising and setting, we remember how life cycles over and over. Tonight the sun sets, tomorrow morning it rises, and on and on. Just as we always return to our breath, to the sunset and sunrise, we always return to our child. And just as our breath and the sun never leave us, neither does our child.

Experiencing Nature

The beauty of this scene
Exceeds my comprehension
Like the beauty of my child

Just as nature has an awesome beauty, so too does your child. And implicit in the comparison is the recognition that just as this Earth's nature offers all types of experiences, pleasant and unpleasant, so too does your child have his own nature, which may sometimes delight and sometimes cause distress. But at the core, your child's nature is one of goodness, joyfulness, and a love that pervades all expressions. Whenever you experience difficulties with your child, reflect on a turbulent nature scene and remember—they are one and the same. Also remember that nature always returns to a state of calm.

Observing Trees

This beautiful scene
Many parents
Many children

Most natural settings across our beautiful Earth are filled with life. Whether the vista upon which we gaze is filled with trees, plants, birds, or other animals, the life forms cross many generations. In the presence of a grove of trees you will find parent trees, children trees, and grandchildren trees. They all stand in harmony and near silence. This verse reminds us that like the trees, we have both parents and children. Contrast the hectic world in which we live with that of the trees standing together in peace. Take a deep breath and imagine all of us slowing down just a little bit, taking a few more deep breaths throughout the day, so that our lives might be as majestic and serene as those of the trees.

Looking at a Full Moon

Beautiful moon
You are always there
So too is my child

When we see a full moon, large against the night sky, we can find ourselves startled by the marvelous beauty of this heavenly body. The moon moves through stages throughout the month, and we sense its changes. But in our lifetime the moon has remained constant. We may take for granted that it is always there, and the important role it plays. It existed long before we were born and it will survive long after we are gone. We might recognize that the love we have for our children is something that is so much greater than ourselves; that it has come from a source that predates us as human beings, and will persist long after our human bodies wither. This verse likens the moon to your child. It invites you to consider whether, from time to time, you take your child for granted, just as you do the moon. It reminds you of the important role your child plays in your life.

Walking

My child's heart beats
With each step I take
Mindfully I touch the Earth
To feel the beats

While we may not realize it, one of the most rhythmic and repetitive acts in which we engage is walking. We develop our gait when we are young, and it remains fairly constant. Walking can become so automatic that we may not even be aware of it. Our child's heartbeat is another natural rhythm we may take for granted. Each time you take a step on this Earth, feel the beating of your child's heart. As you deliberately place each foot down, heel to toe, sense the rhythmic *thump-thump*, so that each footfall represents another beat. A shortened version that may make recitation of this powerful verse easier to do more often is:

With every step I take
My child's heart beats

You may find that it is difficult to slow down to match the pace of a beating heart. Try as we may, our bodies want to speed up. We feel clumsy. We become aware of others watching us. Most of this is in our head. No one cares, or even notices, that we are walking slowly. What's actually happening is that by slowing down, we become more aware of what is happening around us. You will notice leaves flittering on branches, ants crawling on the ground, a gentle breeze caressing your face. You will be surprised to learn what is actually taking place at this moment—to appreciate that your child's heart is beating.

Anytime

Beautiful child
What are you doing now?

This simple verse can be recited anytime your thoughts turn to your child. The question posed can elicit warm feelings. Another simple verse that can be recited anytime you think of your child is:

We are leaves on a tree
Separate and together at the same time

As with the verses on nature, we recognize our oneness with nature. Here, we imagine ourselves as green leaves running along a branch. We are all part of the same organism, yet we are distinct. During those times when we are especially cognizant of our child's independence, this verse further develops our sense of connectedness.

Exercising

My heart pounds inside me
Each beat sounds my child's name

We exercise for many reasons. Perhaps we are interested in losing weight. Perhaps we wish to gain strength. Or we may wish to clear our mind and calm down. One of the more significant changes to our physiology, while we exercise, is that our heart rate increases. At the same time, the fog inside our brain lifts and we see things with a greater clarity. This is a time we take for ourselves, and it is a time that helps us to feel good about ourselves.

While we are not always conscious of it, our heart is always beating. Its continuous and reliable rhythm keeps us alive and enables us to enjoy more time with our children. Let the accelerated heartbeat you experience while exercising remind you of how fortunate you are to be alive, and of your child's presence in your life. Let your mind focus on your heartbeat, and as you attune to it, hear your child's name in its rhythm.

Stretching

Stretching
I send my thoughts to my child
Whose love is as open
As the sea

Stretching, whether through yoga asanas or other methods, opens your body and frees your breath. As you adjust your posture and exhale, open awareness to your child's presence and sense your breath effortlessly moving through space to gently caress your child. Imagine yourself floating with your breath so that you can feel the caress. Sense your child breathing freely and fully and appreciate your child's potential to feel and express love as boundless as the sea.

Important Moments

Birthday Party

My child's birth
My child's laughter
Whose smile is bigger?

Your child's birthday marks a splendid moment. It is an exciting time for them, and it can be a very satisfying time for you. While you celebrate the birthday once a year, you cherish your child's birth—your child's life—all the time. Of course, the birthday party serves as a cue for you to actually take the time to celebrate. This verse is meant to be used not only when you celebrate your child's birth, but when you celebrate any child's birth—or, for that matter, anyone's birth, including your own. Reflect on the joyful smiles and laughter that fill such occasions. Imagine the smile on your child's face, and the smile it brings to your own. Whose smile is bigger?

First Day of School

My child's journey begins
We both will change
With every passing day

Among the many milestones that mark a lifetime, the first day of school is an especially poignant one. It marks the beginning of the formal educational process. The profundity and excitement associated with one's first day of school is such that we probably remember our own, all those years ago. How we have changed! Because attending school quickly falls into a routine, this day marks a special opportunity to appreciate that a journey is about to begin. It is a journey that our children embark on by themselves. And, for the rest of their lives, as they continue to learn, they will continue to grow and change, as will we.

As you prepare for the first day, as you walk with your child into the classroom, and as you listen to your child share her thoughts, feelings, and concerns over what it means to be going to school by herself, breathe deeply and reflect on this wonderful adventure. This verse can be recited every year when the school year begins, and is applicable each time your child embarks on a new experience.

When a Tooth Falls Out

My child's tooth
Where will it be
In a million years?

Our children grow up so fast. While it may seem at first as if they grow up slowly, before long it is clear that they are growing up *too* fast. Mindful parenting helps this natural passage feel more natural and deliberate. We become aware of the time as it passes, and do not merely reflect on it as a bewildering afterthought.

Part of the growing process entails the loss of your child's first set of teeth. It's interesting that we sugarcoat the fact of our child's aging by conjuring a "tooth fairy" who will magically replace the fallen tooth (and our awareness) with a gift or some money. There is no need to eliminate this ritual. Instead, allow it and the circumstances to create an opportunity to mindfully appreciate this wonderful moment. Our bodies are constantly changing. In this life, we age, experience ill health, and eventually pass away. The tooth is a reminder we need not overlook. As you take the tooth in your hand, take the time to feel it, and sense how it once played such an important role in your child's life. Contemplate the gap left behind. And consider, as the verse invites you to, what will become of the tooth in a million years.

While on Vacation

Tomorrow evaporates
And I settle into the stillness
Of my child's smile

We take vacations for a variety of reasons. One common feature of most vacations is that we have an easier time letting go of our need to focus on, or be concerned about, the future. So too, we are less inclined to feel a tug from the past. We breathe a little easier, see more clearly the beauty around us, and more naturally settle into the "now."

Perhaps you are alone or spending time with a few friends in a beautiful locale. You feel the quietude and acknowledge to yourself that you are "in a different place." Your state of mind shifts. Let the stillness of the moment resound deeply as you summon an image of your child's smile. No noise, no hugging, no questions . . . just a peaceful smile.

If you are on vacation with your children, and they are vying for your attention, you can become conflicted as you try to find quiet time to relax or work on some project. At such moments, let the verse awaken you to a realization that there really is no deadline other than one imposed out of habit. Turn to your child and consciously "let go" of the project for a few moments. Look your child in the eye and smile. Give her your full attention. Relaxation is a moment away. The project will not disappear.

Let the verse awaken you to this realization. Tomorrow evaporates because there really is no tomorrow. We just keep moving along the "now." Finding yourself at the crossroad between your personal needs and those of your child, freeing yourself of "tomorrow," liberates you from the constraints of "not enough time." Sink into the stillness of your child's smile.

Mindful parenting does not involve self-sacrifice. Whether or not you are on a vacation, you are the best judge of your decisions on what to do, when to do it, and with whom. The role of mindful parenting is to open yourself up at these moments to your connection with your child. That opening up can take place within the space of a few seconds. At the same time, as you begin to open more, your perceptions of time and your capacity to appreciate the endless quality of every moment ripens.

Looking at Your Child's Creative Work

How beautiful
My child's mind

All that our children produce is an expression of who they are. Their early artwork flows effortlessly from within them and captures our hearts. How beautiful and revealing are these works! As our children mature, the volume of work they produce increases. Do we take it for granted? Are there times that we review it critically and not with open hearts? When we read their words or view their art, let this verse remind us that such expression represents the physical and emotional unfolding of who they are in the cosmos.

Discussing Spirituality with Your Child

This child
Answers all my questions
Let me listen to her questions

A wonderful story tells of a young child who asked his parents if he could spend time alone with his infant baby brother. The parents listened at the door as their little boy approached the crib and said to his infant sibling, "Tell me about God. I am beginning to forget." It is a special time when children ask questions about the mysteries of the universe. Their instincts are always profound.

It is not uncommon for the depth and intensity of feelings we have for our children to illuminate or confirm our own spiritual questions. We play an important role in our children's lives when they begin to ask us such questions. Listen deeply to what your child is asking. Let your responses come from that place within yourself that you share with your child. Breathe deeply and pause for a few moments before answering.

Untying Life's Knots

We live in a complicated world filled with people with complex personalities. And while we would like to think that we have reached a point in our evolution that lifts us above our primitive instincts and urges, they are very much a part of us, and life remains a struggle. If you examine other animals in nature, where the struggle is simply for daily survival, you may observe that while an animal is driven to survive, it does not necessarily feel anxiety as a part of its struggle. The animal lives in the moment, doing what it needs to do to survive. And while I believe that non-human animals possess a great many attributes that we overlook, I think it unlikely that they obsess over past mistakes or fret about future encounters. Furthermore, though they struggle with one another to survive, most animals probably do not find themselves emotionally at odds with other animals, no matter the stakes.

Yet we humans constantly find ourselves in the middle of emotional turmoil and interpersonal conflict.

Such circumstances generally result in our heart racing, our head pounding, and our mind roiling with feelings of stress, disappointment, frustration, disgust, and even rage. At such times, especially when our children are far away, we are not likely to bring them into our awareness and awaken the deep connection we have to the cosmos. Instead, we tend to react by fighting back, or running in fear. While we want to keep our wits about us, we can be so much more effective if we introduce mindfulness to the moment.

Of course, there are many ways we may want to deal with these situations. But one powerful approach is to become more mindful of the moment. In terms of mindful parenting, awareness of our children can be cued during such jarring times. This re-connection with our children can then help awaken us from a mindless state. When we find ourselves involved in a difficult interpersonal interaction, it is a wonderful thing to add a layer of awareness to the moment, thereby bringing our thoughts to our breath and to our child. If done well, while the content underlying the struggle remains, all other factors evaporate; our ego loses its footing. As a result, we become increasingly capable of responding appropriately to the problem at hand. Even if the other person remains lost in the struggle, we single-handedly are able to dissipate the negative emotional charge. It takes two hands to tie a knot, but only one to untie it.

This section looks to those situations in which we find ourselves tied in an emotional knot. If we mindlessly plow through the encounter, it invariably will lead to further emotional anguish and a deeper entrenchment into our positions. But if, at some point during the knot-tying and tightening, we awaken to the reality of what is happening, we can make the decision to step back and untie the knot ourselves. Perhaps the other person will join us; perhaps not. It doesn't matter, because we are doing it for its own sake. The verses in this section look to some of the more general conflict situations in which we may find ourselves, and offer the opportunity to turn to something that is real, something we have pushed to the very back of our mind—our child.

When in a Dispute with Another

I am feeling anger and frustration
Breathing deep, my thoughts turn to my child
Who will one day feel as I do now
May she breathe the anger away from her core

Life is filled with conflict, and quite often, it is difficult to extricate yourself from its powerful grip. But each challenging situation presents an opportunity to undo the tension that holds together that conflict. One method for accomplishing this is to step back and view the problem from a different perspective—that of an observer. In doing so, you might perceive each participant's position differently, and find that you may be more in agreement than you thought you were—that the other person is not being so unreasonable, or that ultimately, the issue upon which the conflict is based is just not that important. To help take this step back, or just to step out of the current of tension, take a deep breath. At the time you take the breath, you shift your focus away from what you are saying or what you are listening to, and root yourself deeper in the present.

Your children likely will engage in a similar pattern of dispute engagement and dispute resolution. Briefly visualize your child caught in a similar situation with a similar choice. Take a deep breath and exhale your anger or frustration with the hope that your child will do the same, and in doing so will find herself a happier person.

Ending a Relationship with Someone Close

I cherish the moments
Not the person
Not myself

Whether you are ending a relationship with somebody, or somebody is ending a relationship with you, rarely is there a sense of joy at this time. Oftentimes, however, the relationship was once full of promise and offered a great deal of joy. We often view ourselves as stationary beings, people and objects coming into and out of view with little we can change because we are stuck where we are. Instead, imagine yourself floating down a river. There are people and objects that float alongside you for a while, and then perhaps bank on the shore or ride a current that passes you by. From this perspective, those people and objects are natural events following nature's flow. Along these lines, when a relationship has ended, it can be an important reminder that you should cherish even that moment, and recognize that the river's flow is a natural one.

Like the river, your child is constantly changing and growing. And as he matures, he will at times be close and at other times distant. As with all relationships, it is the here and now that presents you with your greatest capacity for compassion and joyful expression.

When Your Child Competes with the Television for Your Attention

I am engrossed in waves of color and sound
Coming out of a little box
While the waves of color and sound in front of me
My heart ignores

We so often lapse into states of automatic behavior—mindlessness. While we cannot give our children our full attention all of the time, and as a part of their maturation it is important they understand this, we should be mindful when we choose not to attend to their needs so that the decision is a deliberate one, properly balancing competing interests. Think of how often people find themselves so engrossed in a television show that they ignore their spouse, a parent, or their children. This verse is not intended to suggest which way to turn your attention, but serves to awaken you to what is actually taking place at the moment, so that the decision you make is a thoughtful one.

When Your Child Is with a Babysitter

My child is secure
And will learn
From another

It can be difficult leaving a child with a babysitter. Until the sitter becomes a regular fixture in your lives, or your child adjusts to even having a sitter, the internal tug you feel at the door can be intense. Your child cries out and you leave with mixed feelings. But it is important to be able to leave your child from time to time and have him adjust to the changed environment. When you leave your child, do so fully mindful of your departure. Look at your child and listen to him. When you say good-bye, do so with an open heart. This verse, cued when you are leaving your child with a babysitter, or when he is with a sitter and your thoughts turn to them, is a reminder that your child is his own person and will have an opportunity to learn from another human being.

When Your Child Acts the Contrarian

My child challenges me at every turn
And I find myself engaged in a battle
A slow, deep breath releases an anxious grip
And I listen to my child

It can be very frustrating when your child does not listen to you. But your expectations for your child's compliance may assume a lot about his emotional and mental capacities. While it is important that you establish early on your role as caretaker and decision maker, you owe it to yourself not to create a battle out of thin air. Because of the complex interpersonal dynamic driving your relationship with your child, it is easy to forget that you hold all the cards; you are the powerful one, and ultimately, you can force your child to do whatever you want. He, in contrast, has no power and cannot force you to do anything. He is constantly exploring the parameters of his influence, and you play a fundamental role in his developing sense of himself. This verse helps to assess the situation by reminding you to take a deep breath in order to disrupt the energized state of tension that has arisen and—because you are ultimately charged as a parent with using your power responsibly—to listen deeply to what your child is really saying. It may be necessary to take several deep breaths. You might ask your child to join you in breathing deeply, or you may lovingly announce that you need a few minutes to think about what's going on. Doing so, you can create a more mindful place to deal with what is likely a fleeting state of frustration for both parent and child.

When Your Child Cries

At first your cries may confuse me
But now I feel your heart beating so fast
And I can taste the salt of your tears

Your child may cry for a lot of reasons. The cry may be a plea for attention. Your child may cry because she is scared or injured. Sometimes you are in a ready state, able to understand your child's needs, and to provide for her. At other times, you are distracted and don't fully comprehend your child's needs. This verse directs your attention to something deeper than your child's words. The lines provide a cue to help you become mindful of your child's inner state. There is a heart that is beating faster, tears that are not just drops of water; the salt content in our tears is similar to that of the salt content in the ocean. If you recognize your child's tears for what they are—an expression of Earth's most vital source of life and energy—you can better understand that your child is engaged in a genuine quest for your help and protection.

This does not mean that you should drop everything to attend to your child every time she cries. But if you break away from what you are doing and really listen to your child, you can come to acquire a truer understanding of her needs, and the best means of providing assistance.

When Your Child Is Frustrated to Tears

My child feels alone
Until I take the time
To listen
To the calm within her cries

When your child's cries arise out of deep frustration, he wants desperately to be heard, to be understood. At this moment, words are not available, and a more calm approach is beyond your child's reach. Often we listen to such cries and react with the primary goal of stopping the crying; we are uncomfortable with the sound and our perceptions of our child's distress. Our discomfort may even lead us to become angry if we find ourselves unable to stop the crying; we may be embarrassed, or distracted by competing needs. But if you listen intently to your child, and take a moment to let the sound penetrate into your mind and body, you can sense within the tears and anguish a stillness that transcends the moment, and with which you can deeply identify. Respond to your child from this state of mind and body, and he will know you are listening. You will come to know your child at an even deeper level.

When Your Child Challenges You

In this tug-of-war
I am fighting with myself
If I lose, I win

It is precisely because we are so connected to our children that we can find ourselves mired in a tug-of-war with them. Over time, our children become well equipped to pull the very strings that cause us to pull our hair out. But the battle of wills between you and your child ultimately is an internal struggle. There can be no joy in beating down your child by prevailing in an argument. At the same time, it is important that your child learns to cope in the world, and must not expect you to satisfy every want or need. It is your job to navigate between ceding everything to your child, so as to not diminish their spirits, and meting out harsh rules simply for their own good. This verse can be recited when you find yourself in the middle of a struggle with your child, whether it is at the very beginning, in the middle, or at the end.

Being Interrupted by Your Child

Focusing on myself
My child interrupts me
I breathe deep and listen
To a sound that fades too quickly

One of the complaints most often uttered by parents about their children is that they interrupt them and demand their attention. Among the most difficult tasks of parenting is prioritizing our time so that we bring into balance the time we need for ourselves and the time we devote wholeheartedly to our children. As expressed in the verse, we are interrupted only when we are focused on ourselves. Our child cannot interrupt us when we are truly mindful of him. Mindful parenting helps us to recognize that even these tricky moments are precious, and that one day we may find ourselves wishing to again experience even the most trying of times with our child, simply to be with him. This verse reminds us to take a deep breath and listen to the sound that will fade all too soon, with the realization that all such sounds will one day fade.

When Disciplining Your Child

I am not your enemy
But your protector
You can trust me to feel compassion
Even when I punish you

The verses in this book are not intended to provide parenting instruction or tips. Each parent has their own parenting style and approach to discipline. But no matter the approach, discipline is meted out with some measure of reluctance. It is a time when your child makes it very clear that he is not happy with you. Still, because you are responsible for preparing your child for the "real world," you do your best to put his long-term interests ahead of the expediencies of the moment, and often find yourself utilizing some form of discipline. This verse is a reminder that your actions are guided by a sense of compassion and that you, above all others, are bestowed with the privilege of being your child's protector.

Opening to the Unexpected and to Sadness

We do our best to provide for ourselves, our family, and our community. But life remains a mystery, and unexpected and sometimes unwanted events come our way. These can be times of great disappointment and sadness, and can evoke feelings of anger, sadness, and despair—feelings that will pass as our bodies naturally adjust to the workings of the world. It is at these times that we are likely to find ourselves most vulnerable. Because the unwanted circumstance assumes significant control over our daily routine, we may become especially distant or needy. At these times, mindful parenting can help us to maintain a healthy balance between our personal needs and the needs underlying our relationship with our children and those around us.

Because of the emotional toll taken by the unexpected and unwanted, whether it is of a very limited duration or long-lasting, if we interrupt our feeling state with the space of mindfulness, we enable the expression of joy even at a very sad time in our lives. The benefits of mindful parenting are incremental. By continuing to engage in mindful-parenting practice, we more fully open to the joy within us. Thus, engage in mindful parenting as an end in itself. Do not look to feel better the moment a mindful-parenting verse is thought or uttered, but know deep down that awakening to the present moment while in the midst of inner turmoil cannot help but open you to a greater sense of peace.

A Child's Injury

I cannot absorb all her pain
She is her own person

There is perhaps no greater discomfort a parent can feel than that associated with a child's injury. If the injury is severe, we feel great anguish. But even if the injury is slight or the pain modest, as parents we cannot help but feel our children's pain. This fact speaks to a paradox of existence. On the one hand, we are so connected to our children that we feel their pain. On the other hand, as separate beings, there is nothing we can do to shield our children from feeling pain. Ultimately, the very same reason you cannot shield your child from pain is the very aspect of your child's existence that provides you with the greatest joy. Your child is her own person; her accomplishments are hers alone. And her life's journey, ultimately, is one she takes by herself. It is your job to help her prepare for this journey, to be there for her when she needs you, and then to comfortably let go so that she may experience fully all that life has to offer her.

Consoling Your Child

Following my child's breath
I feel his pain

When your child is upset, you are not always able to make him feel better. But you can always be there for him, truly present to listen to his story, or to sit silently with him as he works through the problem. This verse calls on you to direct your attention to your child's breath. It may be labored, or in some manner disrupted from its normal flow. If you follow your child's breath while maintaining a sense of your own, you can better tune into your child's feeling state.

When Your Child Has a Fever

The warmth I feel
In the palm of my hand
Draws awareness
Into my body

When your child has a fever, you naturally become attentive to your child's needs. Most of the time, the fever passes quickly. But, if it takes a while to resolve, you may find yourself becoming concerned, largely out of the discomfort associated with uncertainty. The best decisions regarding your child's health are made from a state of presence, neither too concerned nor nonchalant.

This verse converts the source of concern—your child's warm body temperature—into an energy state that flows away from your thinking mind and moves into your body. As a result, the same energy that fuels uncomfortable thought patterns is redirected into your hands, facilitating a state of present moment awareness.

Recite the verse when you place your hand on your child's forehead. As you remove your hand, pause and direct attention to your hand. Look at your fingers and, breathing deeply, feel the warmth swirling along your fingertips. This can be a good time to practice the *Twelve-Step Mind-Body Flow Exercise*, found on page 179. Start the flow at your forehead or your hand, whichever you prefer, and, as the exercise instructs, focus awareness on your body working your way down to your feet. Doing so will further release you from uncomfortable and unnecessary thoughts and bring awareness more squarely into the present moment.

Feeling Depressed

Emotions flow through my body
Like clouds across the sky
My love for my child
Resides deep and still within my heart

Life is not always easy, and sometimes we experience difficult emotional ups and downs. This verse contrasts the ebbing and flowing of our emotional well-being with the solidness of our affection for our child. It can be difficult breaking away from intense emotional states, and during emotional turmoil we may not feel motivated to move into a mindful place. For this reason, it can be helpful to recite this verse during calm periods, in preparation for those times that can feel overwhelming.

Seeing an Accident on the Road

I do not always feel another's misfortune
Even though we are all connected
May I always feel
What my child feels

Human beings have interesting ways of dealing with other's misfortunes. Among the most common situations where we confront another's misfortune is witnessing a traffic accident. The accident may be a minor one, one of uncertain consequences, or one involving a fatality. Due to the circumstances of our approaching and leaving the scene, the moment passes quickly and rarely touches us. But, in fact, another person has been placed in a very uncomfortable, if not terrible, situation. Rarely do we take the time to empathize. This verse serves two purposes. First, it invites reflection on the misfortune experienced by another human being. And second, because your child is also another human being, it serves as a powerful reminder that she is vulnerable to this world's forces.

Feeling Sick

My body is feeling sick
No matter what
I take care of my sick child

This verse reminds us of the unconditional love we feel for our children. We don't always take care of ourselves as well as we should. Sometimes we are too busy to do so. Sometimes we don't listen to our bodies, and we fail to detect early signs of emotional or physical distress. But we always listen for these things in our children. Instinctively, we attend to our children's needs with an open heart and alert mind. When you feel sick, this verse reminds you to consider whether you are taking sufficient care of yourself, as you would of your child. Any time you are able to awaken to these feelings and to the naturalness of this compassion, you gain a deeper appreciation for your relationship with your child. You might also take better care of yourself—an important lesson to teach your child.

A Family Member's Passing

A loved one's death reminds me
That flesh and blood return to the Earth
My child is alive
And continues to grow

The passing of a loved one carries with it its own personal difficulties, and may create emotionally touching moments with our children, depending upon their ages and their relationship to the person who has died. No matter how much we accept our mortality, we struggle with these losses. This verse is not intended to affect how we feel at such times. Rather, its aim is to provide a larger perspective from which to experience the loss. Just as our loved one has passed away, so too will we one day pass away.

And, while it is difficult to imagine, one day your child will pass away. But now she is alive, and so are you. If another's passing enables you to be more mindful of your child's aliveness, then it can serve to add meaning to your daily life, and to connect you more deeply with your child.

Part III

Meditations

Journeys to Awakening

Part III Meditations: Journeys to Awakening

MEDITATION EXERCISES

Concentrating on the Breath—Breathing with Your Child 115
Concentrating on the Breath—Breathing with Your Child II 115
Concentrating on the Breath—Blowing Out Birthday Candles 116
Child's Name as Mantra 118
Child's Name as Mantra: Variation with Beads 120
Child's Voice as Mantra 120
Mindfulness Meditation: Watching Thoughts and Feelings 121
Walking Meditation 122
Walking Meditation—Variation 123
Washing Hands 123
Using a Mudra: The Moment of Conception 126
Using a Mudra: Hand-Position Variation 127
Using a Mudra: Introducing a Koan 127
Using a Mudra: Adding a Visualization 128
Mudra in Motion: Impermanence and Love 128
Mudra in Motion Variation: Heart and Hands 131
Loving-Kindness Meditation 132
Sitting with Your Child 135
Cradle Your Child and Listen Deeply 136
Love Your Child like a Rock 138

SELF-GUIDED JOURNEYS

Heart Crossings Journey 141
Inner Animal Journey 143
Your Child's Eyes 144
Your Child Is Your Teacher 144
Best Friends 145

VISUALIZATIONS

Calming Exercise as a Prelude to Visualizations 148
The Flow of Nature 149
Being 152
Meditation on the Vastness of Space in Small Places 157
Child Is the Cosmos 159
Hands and Heart 163
Cleansing the Earth 166

DEVELOPING YOUR MEDITATION PRACTICE

Meditation is one method for helping to quiet your thinking mind. This section contains numerous exercises that may be incorporated into—or help you begin—a formal meditation practice. It also presents visualizations, both self-guided and guided, that you may use to facilitate deeper states of relaxation and further expand your spiritual connection with your child and the universe. As with the verses, it is not suggested that you remember and incorporate all, or even many, of these techniques and exercises. Find just one or two that resonate, and gently open yourself to incorporating them into your daily or weekly practice. It is important not to let the choices serve as distractions. Familiarize yourself with the different offerings. Over time, you can experiment until you find the ones that work best for you. You may find that one or more of the exercises simply helps you to relax. If so, you may wish to treat it as a relaxation technique in preparation for other meditations and visualizations. Also, some of the exercises involve bringing to mind or reciting your child's name. For convenience, in these exercises, reference is made to "my child" as a common denominator, though you may wish to replace it with your child's name.

This section does not seek to present fully each of the meditation methods it introduces. For those that ring truest, you are encouraged to learn more about them. These methods and techniques have been in circulation for thousands of years, and you may experience much joy exploring their roots and experimenting with them outside of a mindful-parenting context. Today, there is easy access to books, videos, CDs, and live workshops that examine and work with these ancient teachings.

Meditation Exercises

Concentrating on the Breath—Breathing with Your Child

Focusing on the breath is a timeless meditation technique. It is also a popular one for those beginning to meditate. Here, this classic exercise is combined with imagery of your child as you focus awareness on your breathing.

Sitting comfortably, begin to relax your body with a series of inhalations and exhalations. Do not try to control your breath. Just allow it to flow naturally. Scan your body for areas that are tight and release them with each exhalation. When you are feeling more relaxed, close your eyes, continuing to direct your awareness to your natural breathing rhythm. Follow your breath for a few cycles and then, when you are ready, on an inhalation, silently contemplate: "My child and I are breathing in." On the exhalation, silently contemplate: "My child and I are breathing out." You may wish to visualize your child breathing with you. Should you do so, visualize your child sitting on your lap, or facing you. Repeat this process for ten minutes.

Concentrating on the Breath—Breathing with Your Child II

This simple variation of the above exercise modifies the silent contemplation. As discussed above, open awareness to your breathing, bringing yourself into a state of relaxation. On the inhalation, silently contemplate: "I am breathing in." On the exhalation, silently contemplate: "My child is breathing out." You may wish to visualize your child exhaling as you exhale. Repeat this process for ten minutes.

As you breathe, open awareness to the cycle of life. Your child follows you in this life, and likely will live on after you have passed away. Your inhaling marks your presence in this world. Your child's exhaling marks your child's continuation in this world. The reality of our impermanence can be infused with tenderness and compassion when we come to understand it deeply. This exercise slowly opens our awareness to more fully appreciating our impermanent nature. Often, as this understanding seeps in at a deeper level, we cherish even more the life we have been given, and resist less the challenges we continue to face.

Concentrating on the Breath—Blowing Out Birthday Candles

A common breathing meditation instruction is to count the breath. This powerful technique uses counting as a means to bringing greater awareness to the act of breathing, and is accomplished by silently thinking or quietly uttering the count with each exhalation. As the meditation begins, the first inhalation helps manifest a state of deeper relaxation and calm. Uttering "one" with the first exhalation keeps the mind attentive to the breath. The process is repeated until the count reaches ten, after which time the count starts over. Powerful as it is, and simple as the instructions are, it is not easy. The count is often forgotten as thoughts rove about. But what is important is that eventually, one returns to the breath. Generally this occurs when one realizes that, in forgetfulness, the count has long since passed ten, or that the count simply stopped altogether, way short of ten. The following exercise incorporates the image of a child's birthday cake, to help keep the mind trained on the counting, and, as a result, the breath.

Upon finding a comfortable position, close your eyes and visualize a birthday cake. As you inhale from your nose, visualize an unlit candle upon which a flame appears. Slowly exhale through your mouth, as if you were blowing out the candle, and think "one." Then, as you inhale, visualize two candles that become lit during the inhalation. Exhaling, you blow out the candles and think "two." Repeat this process until you have ten candles on the cake. Then, either work your way backward or start again with one candle, whichever you prefer.

You should find yourself easing into a state of calm as you begin this meditation. You may find it easier to sustain this meditation if you treat the experience as if it were real. One way to do this is to begin, at the outset, by visualizing your child's smiling face, as if it were your child's birthday. Once you bring this image to mind, smile, and then bring your attention to the candles. Place the candles on the cake in such a way that you can easily identify the number of candles—perhaps two rows with up to five candles in each row. As you inhale, imagine all of the candles coming to flame at the same time. Then, as you exhale, blow out all of the candles. If you like, you may try to keep the length of the out-breath constant. More naturally, though, you will find that the out-breath lengthens slightly as the number of candles increases. This is fine, as it may deepen the meditative state. To further deepen the experience, open your senses to the heat generated by the candle flames and the sweetness of the cake's frosting. You can do this by imagining the palm of one or both of your hands running over the tops of the flames or by imagining the taste of the frosting. In doing so, you shift awareness and energy away from your thinking mind and into your body.

This meditation is particularly beneficial to your daily life when you get in the habit of practicing it during quiet times. You may remember the television commercials that encouraged parents to count to ten when they became frustrated with their children. This is a common suggestion, and one that applies to all frustrating circumstances. The idea, of course, is to create distance between the painful emotional state and one's reaction. Often, with even a brief interlude, the intensity of feeling passes and one is better equipped to deal with the challenging situation. The problem, of course, is that it is not always easy to break away and count to ten. This exercise can be a substitute to this suggested technique. It becomes all the more effective when it is practiced during easy, quiet times, so that when you call upon it to help bring you out of a reactionary state, it is familiar and you are better equipped to do so.

Child's Name as Mantra

A classic meditation technique designed to aid in the development of deepening awareness is the repetition of a mantra. A mantra can be a word, a name of God, or a spiritual phrase that is repeated over and over again. Often it is one that carries no particular meaning to the meditator, and it may derive from a foreign tongue. In this way, the repetition, which is intended to bring the speaker into a deeper and deeper state of concentration and awareness, does not elicit much thought. As discussed in Part I, it can be difficult for many to utilize this technique, as the ego tends to regard exercises that still the mind as boring.

As an alternative to traditional mantra practice, work with your child's name. If your child has (or had) a memorable way of pronouncing their name, consider using it instead. To identify the mantra, spell the letters of your child's name backwards and arrive at a comfortable pronunciation. This conversion is made because repetition of your child's name likely will prove distracting as the name triggers so many different emotions. Because a backward pronunciation generates a different word, few, if any, of the distractions will survive. At the same time, at a level deeper than word comprehension, you will recognize the connection. You will retain deep awareness that you are pronouncing your child's name. That the mantra's closing sound is the first sound of your child's name will not be lost on you.

This technique is helpful because love and compassion are our truest nature. Not surprisingly, it is common for people who experience deep meditative states to report feeling tremendous love and compassion for all beings. You have identified your child's name with a deep and abiding sense of love and compassion from very early in your child's life, perhaps even before birth. When this name is uttered, even backwards, during a state of relaxation and a quiet mind, love and compassion begin to flow naturally, resonating deep inside the core of your being. The challenge is to recite the name without conjuring associated thoughts of your child. In this exercise, the name serves as a connection to love and compassion.

Begin by bringing yourself into a state of calm. Open awareness to your breathing and come to relax into your normal breathing cycle. Clear your mind of thoughts. If thoughts arise, let them pass by like clouds across a night sky. When you are comfortable, close your eyes and begin to inhale through your nose. Gently purse your lips and exhale through your mouth. As you do, softly whisper your mantra. By focusing on this one thought that repeats itself over and over again, you begin to let go of other thoughts, easing your mind of its interminable chattering. If you detect your mind beginning to wander, bring your attention back to your breathing and to your child's name. Repeat this process for ten minutes, or as long as you like.

Child's Name as Mantra: Variation with Beads

To facilitate the ease with which you repeat your mantra, you may wish to use a string of beads. In Eastern meditation, a string of 108 beads—called a mala—is used to fix your mind on the meditation practice. Simply pass the beads across your fingers, reciting the mantra each time you move from bead to bead. If your mind wanders, the presence of the beads will bring you back to the mantra. The beads can also help you keep track of the hour, should you wish to time your meditation without the concern of looking at a timepiece.

Child's Voice as Mantra

Instead of using your child's name as a mantra, you may use the sound of your child calling you. It is generally not difficult to conjure the sound of your child calling you "Mommy" or "Daddy." If you are able to do so, then follow the instruction above for "Child's Name as Mantra," with or without the use of beads, repeating this sound over and over in your mind's ear. You may find it easier to establish this rhythm by reciting the first syllable on the inhalation and the second syllable on the exhalation. In this way, you hear *mah* on the in-breath and *mee* on the out-breath; *da* on the in-breath and *dee* on the out-breath. After a short while, you may find that the sound of your child's voice fades as you continue to ride the waves of your breathing.

Mindfulness Meditation: Watching Thoughts and Feelings

A common misconception about meditation is that thoughts are bad or undesirable, and that the goal of meditation is to eliminate all thoughts. To the contrary, many schools of meditation appreciate the natural arising and passing of thoughts and do not seek to suppress or rise above this phenomenon. What matters is that there is awareness of the arising and passing of thoughts. This is to say that we are mindful of our body, mind, and emotional state. For example, if, while sitting in meditation, your ear itches, the miracle of mindfulness presents itself if you recognize that your ear is itching. This stands in sharp contrast to immediately scratching the ear, perhaps out of habit and in complete disregard for what is taking place. So too, if a feeling state of envy arises, become aware that you are feeling envy. Try not to get lost in the moment and carried away by the feeling. Mindfulness creates space between you and the feeling state.

A popular technique is to name or note whatever arises during the meditation. The mindscape of a typical ten-minute meditation may go something like this: "Feeling distracted—feeling cold—anxiety arising—sexual thought—feeling bored—thinking of tomorrow—urge to get up—still feeling cold." Each time a feeling state is noted, you return to your breath, or to whatever object forms the basis of the meditation.

The mindful-parenting application of this fundamental technique is to imagine sitting with your child, your attention drawn to open space, perhaps a blue sky. You imagine your child holding a megaphone. Together you simply watch for what emerges.

As feeling states arise, you observe your child shouting their name through the megaphone. Should you feel a wave of lethargy, your child raises the megaphone and shouts the word *tired*, or *Mommy is feeling tired.* After you hear this, smile and return to the open sky. Perhaps you will feel silly doing this. Your child shouts *feeling silly*, and you return your awareness to the open sky. In this exercise, your child's presence refines the expansiveness of your thinking mind. Rest your awareness on your child, who will do the hard work for you. Simply be open to what arises. You may hear *there's anger*, *feeling scared*, and *very sad.* Smile as your child holds your hand through this process, helping you to convert ephemeral feeling states into the awareness of feeling states.

Walking Meditation

In addition to the sitting meditation, walking meditation can be very powerful. Because walking is something we do so often, it is worthwhile to explore more fully how it might be incorporated into a mindful-parenting practice. Let's consider the verse on walking, found on page 84.

With every step I take, my child's heart beats.

As discussed more fully in the commentary accompanying this verse, walking meditation can help to slow down the mental chatter taking place in your mind, perhaps driving you to distraction. You can engage in this simple meditation with the first steps you take upon waking in the morning, to help ground you as you start your day. You can also do so while walking into an important or challenging situation, where it may quell the storm of thoughts racing through your mind so that you can focus more easily and be present for the encounter.

Walking Meditation—Variation

An easy variation to the walking meditation is to replace the verse with the silent contemplation you are using when concentrating on the breath. In so doing, you focus on the breath with each step. These contemplations are found in the exercises set forth in subsections one and two above. If you are silently contemplating, "My child and I are breathing in" and "My child and I are breathing out," then recite one part with each step, such that each step represents either an inhalation or an exhalation. You probably will find it necessary to slow down in order to do this exercise. Slowing down will help expand your awareness to the here and now. If you find yourself feeling self-conscious while walking slowly, remember that it is sufficient that you do this for just a few steps. What is most important is that you "wake up" to the present moment. It takes but one mindful step for that to happen.

Washing Hands

I find this exercise to be among the most profound. This is probably the case because it involves a routine act that is repeated many times throughout the day. As a result, if the exercise nudges you out of a state of forgetfulness and into one of beautiful awakening, then its impact can be significant. On top of that, the exercise elicits many different sensory states. As described below, and elsewhere in this book, the convergence of multiple sensory states serves to bring about a richer experience. In this regard, the process of washing hands is one in which temperature (of the water), smell (of the soap), touch (of the fingers to the water, the soap, and each other), and sound (your voice) converge. As discussed below, two additional factors (mindful consumption and expanded consciousness) play a role in further enriching the meditative quality of the experience.

The exercise is very simple. Sing or hum "Happy Birthday" to your child as you wash your hands. If your child's name were Millie, it would go like this:

Happy Birthday to you
Happy Birthday to you
Happy Birthday, dear Millie
Happy Birthday to you

When you finish, bring to mind an image of your child, as he or she appears today. Sense your child smiling and happy, as if you were celebrating a birthday. As set forth below, the exercise contains a few additional elements that serve to slow down the process and open awareness to what is actually happening. If you finish the song before you've finished washing your hands, repeat it as many times as you like. There is no reason to hurry. To the contrary, as discussed in the related verse on "Washing Hands," this is an extraordinary time to slow down and really enter the here and now. Just stand still. In doing so, you will realize how much time you spend in motion.

Begin by turning on the faucet and applying soap to your hands. Then, turn the faucet off. As you turn off the faucet, consider the natural resources you are saving with this simple act. This constitutes mindful consumption, as you deliberately help to conserve the Earth's resources. Slowly begin to massage the soap into your hands, paying attention to how it feels against your palms, fingers, and the tops of your hands. Over time, you will experience a deepening awareness of what it means to truly feel your hands. Then, bring your hands to your nose and inhale the soapy aroma. As with every experience, note how only a few seconds earlier you may have been oblivious to this aroma, emanating from just a few inches away. Take this opportunity to inhale fully, expanding your belly and then exhaling. Slow down and do this twice. No matter how prolonged the hand-washing is, it will not take more than a minute. Then, look down at your hands. If there are suds, notice how the size of the round bubbles vary. Sense the bubbles as planets and stars, filling the galaxy. There, before you, is the cosmos. And in the same space, are your hands. This is expanded consciousness. You become aware, simultaneously, of the vastness of the universe and of your own presence. As you turn on the water, feel its wetness as it flows over your hands, cleaning away the dirt and germs that had accumulated. Look deeply into your hands as the water rushes over them, and marvel over your creation.

By this time, you should have finished a chorus of "Happy Birthday" and be visualizing your smiling child. Place your hands on top of one another so that the water flows from one to the other like a waterfall. Sense you and your child playing together at the bottom of the waterfall. You have washed your hands tens of thousands of times in your lifetime. You can now begin to transform this routine experience into one of great profundity. Every sink, wherever situated, becomes a sanctuary.

This exercise can also be a good gauge of your current state of presence. The exercise takes a matter of seconds—surely a trivial allotment of time. Still, there may be the sensation of not having enough time (or you may feel too distracted) to take the twenty-odd seconds to wash your hands in mindful awareness. A gentle nudge to wash again in case you flew through the process in forgetfulness is always helpful. In such cases, there can be joy in having caught yourself and woken up just in time. But, should you not have the interest or find that you completely forgot until much later, then rest comfortably in the knowledge that there is a deeper place of presence within, and that, for the rest of your life, you will have renewed opportunities to move into this space.

Using a Mudra: The Moment of Conception

In the Buddhist tradition, *mudras* are hand positions that can invoke inner states of experience and energy. Many spiritual traditions coordinate hands and fingers in a variety of positions to steady and deepen the practice. As such, these mudras commonly play a role in meditation. A classic mudra for sitting meditation, representing spaciousness, is the gentle touching together of thumb and index finger (or thumb and forefinger). The traditional pose is to sit with your arms draped along the top of your thighs, or, if you are sitting in a chair, on its armrests. In this exercise, the touching together of thumb and finger represents the moment of your child's conception—the union of egg and sperm. This imagery is intended for both birth and adoptive parents, as the moment of your child's conception, wherever it took place, began the wondrous transformation of your life.

As you sit with your hands forming this mudra, consider one of your hands. Gently rub your fingers together, and then, allowing them to separate ever so slightly, sense the space between the tip of your thumb and the tip of your finger, between egg and sperm at that precarious moment just prior to your child's conception. Direct your awareness into this space. Bring yourself into a state of deeper calm by breathing into and out of this gap. Periodically touch together thumb and finger to stimulate this profound awareness. You may notice a tingling sensation along the nerve endings of your fingertips. Periodically check your breathing to ensure that it is slow and regular.

Using a Mudra: Hand-Position Variation

Another mudra, commonly referred to as the meditation mudra, involves resting your hands together in your lap, the right hand cradling the left, thumbs lightly touching. This exercise is the same as the one above. The only difference is that the point of conception resides between the two thumbs.

Using a Mudra: Introducing a Koan

When you find yourself stable in this posture, contemplate:

Where was my child before she was born?

This question is similar to a Zen *koan*—such as "What is the sound of one hand clapping?" A koan (pronounced kO´An) is a device used in Zen meditation, designed to introduce unanswerable questions that confound the mind to the point of expanded awareness. Just sink into a state of awareness, centered on the profound nature of the question. As an alternative, you may wish to ponder:

Where was my love for my child before she was born?

Breathing steadily, this meditation will bring you deeper and deeper into stillness.

Using a Mudra: Adding a Visualization

Using either hand position, you may wish to add a visual element to the meditation. Doing so may enhance the sensation of the meditation or help bring about a deeper penetration into stillness. The visualization introduces a beautiful setting, such as a forest, lake, sky, mountain range, ocean, or any other scene that comes to mind during the meditation. With the question "Where was my child before she was born?" floating in your consciousness, look to the space between thumb and finger and visualize or sense the scene in your mind's eye. After one or more breaths, when you are ready, move from this setting to another—perhaps from a beautiful forest to a vast expanse of ocean—and again, bring awareness to the question. With each breath, open to another scene upon which to ponder your child's essence prior to conception.

Mudra in Motion: Impermanence and Love

This exercise takes a little practice, but you will find the fruits well worth the effort. Unlike the previous mudras—which involve meditating around a relatively fixed hand position—in this one, you set your hand in motion. You can practice moving mudras most any time—while waiting at a traffic light, while on "hold," sitting in a business meeting, taking a break from the computer, while engaged in a challenging interpersonal interaction, in the bath or shower, or just before bedtime. As you will observe, this mudra expresses powerful emotional content. By developing a greater familiarity and comfort with the impermanence of all that is, you will come to respond more deftly to the change inherent in all experience.

Begin by extending before you your dominant hand. While in practice you may alternate hands, or even use both at the same time, it's a good idea to start with this hand in order to maximize your ability to quickly incorporate the motor skills and movements involved.

Steps One and Two: Nothingness and Conception

Start by squeezing your hand in a tight ball. As you squeeze out the air and eliminate the space, sense the stillness and quietude. Then, slowly release your grip and touch together your index (middle) finger and thumb, so that an "O" is formed. Allow the other fingers to naturally follow the curve. This particular posture is known as the "Aakaash" mudra, and is associated with space. Breathe deeply and expand your belly. Feel the inner spaciousness.

Look at your hand—and the "O" you've formed—and sense the vast expanse of the cosmos. In this exercise, your thumb symbolizes the mother's egg (ovum), and the middle finger symbolizes the father's sperm. Their touching represents the moment of your child's conception. Breathe deeply and sense this magnificent moment.

Steps Three and Four: Childhood and Adulthood

Continue to open your hand, moving your thumb downward and lifting the fingers, but keeping the fingers curved as long as you can. As your fingers slowly open and eventually straighten (so that your hand forms an "L"), you sense in your mind's eye your child crawling, and then standing upright, as an adult. At some point during this hand movement, you may pass your child's current age. If you do, mark the moment with a smile. When your hand is fully extended in the "L" position, visualize your child as an adult.

Step Five: Adulthood and Aging

If you find the following step emotionally difficult, you may want to skip over the next two hand movements and proceed directly to Step Seven. However, the next two sections are very heart-opening, and may serve to enrich your meditation.

Keeping your thumb extended, slowly curve your fingers back down, stopping about halfway so that a "C" is formed with your hand. This movement represents your child's aging, the curve symbolizing your child's stooping spine as he or she grows into old age.

Step Six: Aging and Death

From the "C" position, slowly extend your fingers upward so that an "L" is re-formed, and then turn your hand over, stretching it back so that it fully extends, forming a 90-degree angle with your forearm. This symbolizes the end of your child's life on this Earth. Take a deep breath, inhaling and exhaling fully. Rest on the exhalation for a few seconds.

Steps Seven and Eight: Completing the Cycle

Slowly, move your fingers and thumb toward each other, but this time, do not stop and form an "O." Instead, continue closing your grip and form a fist. Squeeze. Then, release the grip, but keep your fist intact. Breathe deeply, and slowly bring your hand back into the starting "O" position.

This completes this exercise on impermanence. Along with all living things, our child's presence on this Earth is in constant transition. To embrace this reality is to be present for the truth of existence. While we hope that the course of our life's events proceeds as the poet suggests in the commentary to the verse, "Reading a Book," found on page 79, the lessons to be learned by embracing impermanence extend far and wide.

Mudra in Motion Variation: Heart and Hands

This variation to the *Mudra in Motion* exercise enhances your sense of connection to your child. It introduces the beautiful image of a heart, created by the ultimate union of both hands. The Mindful Parent website demonstrates this mudra. You can view it by visiting http://themindfulparent.org/mudra/.

The instructions up through the end of Step Six are identical to those set forth in the primary *Mudra in Motion* exercise, except that both hands engage in the same motion simultaneously. The second hand represents you and your presence alongside your child. As you become facile with the movements, you may intuitively stagger the timing between the two hands to mark the difference between you and your child's ages and stages of development. At the conclusion of Step Six, with both arms outstretched in the position of an upside-down "L," bring both of your arms together so that they meet, forming a "T." The palms, fully extended in opposite directions, form the top bar of the "T." If this position calls for too much of a stretch, you may allow your forearms to separate, always ensuring that the base of your palms remain pressed together.

Then, slowly curve the fingertips on both hands toward each other. Just as they are about to touch and form an "O," bring them in toward your palms so that they form a heart shape, touching together about halfway between fingertips and palms.

Pause and take a deep breath. Consider what a beautiful gift it is that you and your child are together in this lifetime. Every moment is a moment together, filled with love, amid this wondrous cosmos.

Loving-Kindness Meditation

As noted in Part I, a mindful-parenting adjustment to a timeless practice can be found in the loving-kindness meditation. This meditation begins by wishing for yourself safety, happiness, health, and a life filled with ease of heart. It is important to be good to yourself and to treat yourself with compassion. For some, this is easy; for others, it is difficult. We introduce our child to this meditation both to make the recitation more comfortable and to enhance our connection to our child. This meditation involves three recitations. In the first, you send loving-kindness to you and your child:

May my child and I be safe
May my child and I be happy
May my child and I be healthy
May my child and I live with ease of heart

Consider replacing my child with your child's name. This simple verse can be recited at any time: upon waking in the morning, upon seeing or thinking about your child, or during the course of sitting or walking meditation. As noted below in the introduction to self-guided journeys, you may also recite the above if you begin to feel uneasy. Try it now and bring to mind your child's image, or sense your child's presence. Among the many different methods, you may enjoy reciting each line silently to yourself while inhaling and exhaling. Using this method, the meditation takes place over two full breaths. An alternative is to softly sound out each line on the exhalation. This method takes four full breaths. If you pick a method that feels right and stick with it, you will more easily find the natural expression of the meditation.

Next, send loving-kindness to your child. For example, when I send loving-kindness to my daughter Rose, I bring her image to mind and recite:

May Rose be safe
May Rose be happy
May Rose be healthy
May Rose live with ease of heart

The juxtaposition of the first two recitations speaks to you and your child's united yet also separate identities. Just as the ocean and sandy shoreline unite when waves break, so, too, do they stand apart when the waves recede. It is a never-ending dance of nature that also plays itself out in your relationship with your child. Sometimes you feel very close; at other times, you feel quite distant. There are occasions when you want nothing more than to spend time with your child. At other times, you need space. The ocean and shore do not resist this phenomenon, and neither should you.

In the third recitation, imagine your child sending loving-kindness to you. Sense your child's presence, using imagery, sound, or both, and listen to your child recite:

Mommy (or Daddy), may you be safe
Mommy (or Daddy), may you be happy
Mommy (or Daddy), may you be healthy
Mommy (or Daddy), may you live with ease of heart

This can be a touching meditation as you and your child exchange (or share) roles. Here your child is wishing for your safety and protection. Of course, as time continues on its never-ending journey, the roles played by parents and children evolve. This recitation reminds us of this natural progression.

You may stop the loving-kindness meditation at this point, or continue in the traditional manner by extending wishes of safety, happiness, health, and living with ease to others. If you choose to continue, start with a benefactor or someone for whom you have deep feelings and regard—someone who makes you smile when you think of them. Then, bringing their image to mind, recite aloud or to yourself:

We wish for you safety
We wish for you happiness
We wish for you health
We wish for you a life lived with ease of heart

Of course, the "we" represents you and your child. At this point, move on to a friend, then a person for whom you have neither positive nor negative regard. Then, recite the meditation to someone who challenges you. And finally, recite it to all beings, everywhere:

We wish that all beings are safe
We wish that all beings are happy
We that all beings are healthy
We wish that all beings live with ease of heart

By expanding the reach of the expressions beyond yourself and your child, you further open your heart and generate compassion. Such expression, especially in regard to one who challenges you, does not imply that you condone another's improper behavior. It simply means that you appreciate that when another being feels safe, happy, and healthy, and lives with ease of heart, they are more likely to act in appropriate and loving ways. It is this which you wish to encourage, and to which you wish to contribute.

Sitting with Your Child

A wonderful exercise is simply to sit across from your child, each of you gazing into each other's eyes. You can sit in chairs, or if you have meditation cushions, on them. This can be a wonderful way to introduce your child to meditation. Nothing is supposed to happen, and there are no rituals to perform. Just sit in silence and watch each other. The only rule is that you try to honor silence for the time allotted. The only thing to expect is spontaneous smiling. The sensation of deep presence inherent in this moment powerfully attests to the depth of connection you share with your child. This is so, even if it lasts but a minute or two. Not surprisingly, this exercise may be difficult to coordinate if your child is too young or too old. If your child is reluctant or resistant, do not persist. There is always the delightful alternative of gazing at your sleeping child.

Cradle Your Child and Listen Deeply

When you are in a meditative state, you experience a falling away of judgments, hopes, and fears. As a result, you become available for whatever arises. Many of the techniques that have been described in this section help to bring about a more mindful, meditative state of being. I learned a variant of the following exercise from a wonderful therapist, Rick Brown, who introduces it to couples as a tool to help them enhance the "consciousness" of their relationship. I find that when it is applied in the parent-child context, it can help one move into a place of meditative awareness.

This exercise involves cradling your child in your arms and listening deeply. With the lights turned low and outside sounds minimized, rest your child's head on your lap. You will want to be sitting, perhaps resting against a wall, as you position your child's head so that the two of you can easily make eye contact. When comfortably in this position, embrace your child, gaze into her eyes, and say "Tell me about your day."

When in a meditative state, it is natural to listen deeply. But deep listening can be challenging much of the time. To help you do this, you will *mirror* your child's answers. This means that whatever your child says, you will simply repeat it. If, for example, your child says, "I go to school," then, when your child finishes speaking, say, "You go to school." Then ask, "Is there more?" It is as if you are a flat mirror, repeating, without filtering or altering in any way, everything your child says to you. This is an opportunity to truly listen to your child and, more importantly, for your child to feel truly heard. When your child says there is nothing more, then proceed by sharing with your child that what she said *makes sense* to you. To do this, you need not agree with what you've heard. Just say, "Well, that makes sense," and explain in simple terms why what you heard makes sense. For example, if your child said that she goes to school, that the teacher is nice but is sometimes strict, and that sometimes she doesn't like the teacher, you can respond, "Well, that makes sense. When you are in school and your teacher is not acting nice, you don't like him." Then, after *validating* your child's expression in this way, *empathize* by saying, "I can imagine that that could make you feel . . ." In this case, you might say that you imagine it could make her feel "unhappy, frustrated and scared."

You may stop here or, if you like, move deeper and ask, "What is the hardest part of your life?" Again, no matter what your child says, simply mirror it. And again, when you finish mirroring ask whether there is more. As before, when your child has no more to say, validate your child by telling her *why* what she said makes sense. Then, embrace her with empathy by sharing how you can imagine it makes her feel.

The purpose of this exercise is not to deal with the content of the subject matter your child raises—that can be done another time. Here you are only interested in listening to your child and mirroring what you hear. There is no problem to solve. There is no lesson to teach. By following the mirroring script set forth above—mirror, validate, and empathize—you will act much the same as if you were truly present. In so doing, you will move into a state of deep presence.

You will probably find the mirroring process to be awkward at first as you let go of thoughts and refrain from commentary. To be *present*, is to listen so deeply that your child intuitively appreciates that she has been truly heard. With a little practice, the mirroring process will proceed with ease and, in time, you will begin to "awaken" to your reactivity and become mindful of what is actually taking place before you.

Love Your Child like a Rock

The cover photograph is of an Inuit carving titled *Mother and Child.* There is beauty and grace in the grounded silence inherent in this artwork. The various meditation techniques contained in this book all serve to bring you closer to a grounded state of deep presence. The changes they effect take place slowly, and proceed at a pace aligned with your own personal evolution. In time, you move ever so much closer to a state of stillness, one which you beckon forth from within as needed. The state of stillness—pure awareness—is often ascribed to a rock. In stark contrast to many people who have difficulty slowing down, the rock is always still. Even when we try to slow down, the urge to return to a faster pace persists. This is often experienced in walking meditation. But when you slow your pace, you begin to observe things differently. Indeed, the vantage point of a rock is extraordinary because it misses nothing.

This exercise involves finding a small rock. It can be one you pick up while on a trip to a relaxing or beautiful spot. Or it can be one you find in a local park, the beach, or even in the gravel of your driveway. You may want to ask your child to pick out a rock for you that he or she finds special. When you select the rock, hold it in your hand and gaze at it for a few minutes. Feel its weight in your palm. Breathe deeply and slowly and intuit that portion of yourself that knows stillness—that moves toward quiet and peace.

Place the rock on a table or counter in your home and let it serve as a mindfulness cue. Whenever you notice it, consider whether you are moving or thinking too fast. You may want to reach out and touch it to charge your mindfulness cells. Assess whether the thoughts running through your head are of the moment, or instead deal unnecessarily with the past or future. Stand still and, if possible, stop talking, even if for only a second. Listen deeply, whether to your child, to whomever you may be speaking, to the thoughts in your head, or to the sounds surrounding you. Breathe deeply and become the rock.

On those occasions that you find yourself having a difficult time, glance over to the rock and smile. Allow awareness of the rock's stillness to help bring you into the present moment. You need not solve any problems to become present. But when you are present, the challenges problems pose are seen with clarity and you more easily recognize the solutions that manifest. What a gift this ancient piece of Earth provides. You can use this moment of awareness as an opportunity to exercise the *Twelve-Step Mind-Body Flow Exercise* set forth in Appendix A. All this can be accomplished in the flash of thirty seconds. But so much can take place within the span of those thirty seconds.

Self-Guided Journeys

Whereas the above meditation exercises do not naturally invoke visualizations or multiple sensory experiences, the following self-guided journeys do. As you will see, self-guided journeys are a hybrid of the meditations discussed above and the guided visualizations that follow. Unlike guided visualizations, which allow you to passively absorb the content and imagery presented, the flow and content of self-guided journeys are generated by you, spontaneously. You are provided with a general theme that sets the stage for the journey. Because they take on a life of their own, each journey may leave the profound imprint of a real experience. For this reason, if you are able to relax into the process so that spontaneous imagery might flow unfiltered, these journeys offer the promise of deep insight. This insight is something you may wish to explore in your sitting meditation. If at any time during a journey you feel uncomfortable or anxious, or perhaps something disturbing enters the visualization, take a deep breath and recite the loving-kindness meditation: "May my child and I be safe. May my child and I be happy. May my child and I be healthy. May my child and I live with ease of heart." This recitation will help settle any uncomfortable thoughts and allow you to continue with the journey feeling relaxed and spacious inside.

Heart Crossings Journey

As with sitting meditation, find a comfortable position and bring yourself into a state of calm. Close your eyes as the journey unfolds in your mind's eye, much like a movie. Because it is the heart above all other organs that experiences this journey, it is unimportant whether you are particularly good at visualization. The other senses, such as sound, smell, taste, and touch, also factor in prominently.

When you are relaxed, imagine holding your child's hand. Your child can be any age—past, present, or future. On this journey, you are taking your child to meet a loved one who has passed away—preferably someone whom your child did not have the opportunity to meet and who did not get to know your child. It can be a grandparent, parent, sibling, benefactor, close friend, or anyone who played an important role in your life.

Start the journey by looking your child in the eyes and telling him who you are about to visit. If you like, let him know a little about the person and why she is important to you. Then, prepare to visit this special person. You can sense yourself in a room with her, or, if you prefer, fly with your child to wherever she lived. If you live in Miami and this special person lived in Paris, then imagine holding your child's hand as together you lift off the ground and fly to Paris. Try not to rush through these visualizations. You are making it up as you go, so enjoy it. Trust in your heart to guide you through this process.

When you greet the person, introduce her to your child. You may find yourself saying to your grandmother, "Grandmother, this is my daughter, Millie. I wanted Millie to meet you because you were so special in my life. Millie was named after you." Then, perhaps, your child will give your grandmother a hug. Then she may speak to your grandmother. You will delight in what emerges. Your heart will sing. Just let it happen. A conversation may ensue. You may be a part of it, guiding it. You may just sit back and watch. Witness where the journey takes you. When you are ready to leave, you can say your good-byes, and that you'll come back again sometime soon. A pleasant way to end a journey is to sit quietly, imagining that you are holding your child's hand, that your child is holding the loved one's hand, and that the loved one is holding your hand. When you are ready, return to where you first held your child's hand and rouse yourself from the visualization, or, if you wish, visit someone else. This journey can be as long or as short as you like. People have reported deep experiences in which they wonder if perhaps some contact isn't being made after all. Whether or not that is the case, the meditation can awaken deep emotions, evoke insight, and open your heart.

Inner Animal Journey

This next self-guided journey also begins by making yourself comfortable and bringing yourself into a state of calm. Close your eyes and breathe deeply. Then, imagine that you and your child are each a non-human animal. If you have previously considered yourself to be like a certain animal, become that animal. If not, then ponder what kind of animal you are like, or breathe deeply and allow an animal's image to come to mind. Place yourself in the natural habitat of that creature, yourself as the parent and your child as the offspring. Then, journey together. Do not rush the experience. You have nowhere to go. Explore with your child flying, swimming, standing motionless, running, climbing, and the gamut of natural experiences that might take place. Should you encounter any difficulties, recite the loving-kindness meditation. The animal's nonverbal nature can transform the visualization as you begin to communicate at the level of genuine presence.

Your Child's Eyes

In this journey you see yourself through your child's eyes. When you do, compassion and love flow in a very natural way, but one that may be surprising, given the identities and roles in which we typically immerse ourselves. For instance, you probably view yourself as your child's protector, continually carrying the responsibility of ensuring your child's safety and well-being. In this self-guided journey, you release this role.

Bring yourself into a calm and relaxed place—eyes closed, breathing steady. Then, visualize your child gazing lovingly at you. As you gaze back, sense yourself resting inside a baby's cradle. The sheets are soft and comfortable. You cannot speak. In this visualization, you are your child's baby sibling. Your child may be young or old. Allow the journey to flow its natural course. You may want to gaze at each other in silence. Or, perhaps your child has something to say to you. A variation of this journey, which you may want to try, is to view yourself as your child's child.

Your Child Is Your Teacher

Children can be very wise, and when we are open to receiving this wisdom, we can learn a great deal from our children. This journey places your child in the role of teacher. Often, you may be aware of the source of your pain and the basis for self-imposed limitations, but you don't seem to have the strength to overcome these obstacles. This journey sets in motion your desire to acquire a deeper insight into the roots of obstacles and to work through them with greater facility.

Begin by bringing yourself into a state of calm and relaxation. With your eyes closed, visualize your child, however old, standing at the front of a classroom. You are sitting in a chair in the back row, and your child is not aware of your presence. Your child asks whether there are any questions, and there is a moment of silence. Breathing deeply, you call to mind an issue that is troubling you, and formulate it into an open-ended question. For example, you might formulate, "Why am I so _______?" or "Is there a reason I am feeling so _______?" The question may involve your relationship with your child, or it may relate to any other aspect of your life. You see several hands raised, and your child calls on someone. You hear that person pose your question to your child. Just as your child begins to answer the question, change his or her outfit to a kind that you associate with wisdom or compassion. Then, breathe deeply as you listen to your child respond. Your child may choose to write on a chalkboard, play a video or audio recording, or draw on some other external source to help answer the question. If you have any follow-up questions, imagine the same person, or another person, asking them. When the time comes that you choose to conclude the journey, remain in your seat as the classroom empties. When the last person leaves, approach your child and express your heartfelt thanks for helping you find greater clarity in your life.

Best Friends

As with all self-guided journeys, begin by making yourself comfortable and bringing yourself into a relaxing state. In this journey, you are your child's age. You live in a distant city and are visiting. You child is very excited that you are coming, and when you see each other you greet each other as good friends. You are glad to be visiting and excited about where your friend will take you, and what you will explore together. Breathe deeply as you let your child lead the way.

A powerful variation is to have your child join you in your childhood. Perhaps there were times that were especially challenging or particularly wonderful. Invite your child to accompany you as you revisit these moments. Share experiences with your child and, if times were difficult, look to your child for guidance, insight, and compassion. If these early experiences were traumatic, you can choose to visit as observers, watching what transpires from a safe place. Perhaps you will view things with a different perspective. Feel free to change the course of events in your journey, or to provide closure where circumstances may have remained uncomfortably open-ended.

Visualizations

Mindful-parenting visualizations use visual imagery and other sensory experiences incorporating our children that guide us into the stillness that is present in every moment. It is from within this stillness that love and joy explode not just into our hearts, but throughout our entire being. The following visualizations connect us deeply with our children in ways that transcend thought. As with many of the verses, these meditations direct our awareness to our bodies and our children's bodies. As the energy that feeds our repetitive thinking is redirected toward the body, we more easily open into stillness. We emerge from them feeling refreshed and soothed.

There are several ways to enjoy these visualizations. You may want to have someone read them to you slowly. This can be a peaceful and fulfilling interaction. If you would like to listen to them but it is difficult to find someone to read them, or you want to listen to them at odd times or places that do not lend themselves to each interaction, you may record them and then listen to the recording. Be sure to read them much slower than you might otherwise, as the passage of time is much slower when one is in a meditative state. I have created CDs with some of these visualizations. To order these, see the contact information in the back of this book. You can also read each visualization, taking the time to experience the sensory imagery it provokes in your mind's eye. After reading through a visualization once or twice in this way, you can try to conjure the visualization. Do so without thinking about it; just allow sensory impressions to arise. If you find yourself veering off into unknown territory, go with it and see where it takes you.

In order for these visualizations to penetrate deeply, it is helpful to be in a relaxed state as you experience them. Rather than set off each of the following visualizations with a similar set of calming instructions, a general Calming Exercise is presented below. Instructions contained in a visualization to relax or calm down refer to the following exercise. Also, to help with the timing and spaces of silence that penetrate the visualizations, markers are provided that instruct you to either pause for five to 15 seconds (represented by ". . .") or for longer lengths of time (represented by "pause for one minute").

Calming Exercise as a Prelude to Visualizations

Wear loose-fitting clothing and take care that the temperature is comfortable. If it is too cold, consider draping a blanket around you. Sit in a comfortable position, hands resting in your lap or by your side. If you prefer, lie down on your back, with a pillow supporting your knees. Try not to be too comfortable or you may fall asleep. When you are comfortable with your body position, begin paying attention to your breath, observing each inhalation and exhalation. If it is not difficult, breathe through your nose. Sense the air flowing into your nostrils. Sense the air flowing out of your nostrils. Should thoughts enter your mind, smile—and on each exhalation, imagine them blowing away, far off into the distance. There is no need to attend to the thoughts. By keeping your awareness on your breath, you will defuse the energy behind these thoughts. Do this for four breath cycles. You are now ready to scan your body so as to relax more fully.

As each part of your body is identified, visualize and breathe into it. If it feels tight, clench the muscles surrounding it for a few seconds and then let go. Remember to breathe.

Relax the muscles of your face—your forehead, eyes, cheeks, jaw, and throat. Relax your neck and shoulders. Drop your shoulders if you can. Relax your arms and fingers. Relax your chest and your spine. Breathing deeply, relax your stomach, hips, and pelvis. Release any tension in your legs, feet, and toes.

You should now feel a general sense of calm resonating through your whole body. If you feel residual anxiety, repeat this exercise.

The Flow of Nature

Bring yourself into relaxation with the Calming Exercise found on page 148. The following visualization involves you, your child, and nature. While the introduction of each image begins on either an inhalation or an exhalation, do not worry about perfectly coordinating the imagery with your breathing. Just keep your breathing slow and steady and allow the imagery to flow through you. If thoughts begin to interrupt the meditation, simply observe that fact and let it slip away.

* * *

Breathing in, you see you and your child standing at the base of a large mountain. You smell the fresh Earth and feel loose dirt at your feet.

Breathing out, you take your child's hand and together begin to climb the mountain.

Breathing in, you see you and your child standing before a beautiful lake.

Breathing out, you and your child step into the lake. You feel the cool water breaking at your ankles. You hold your child's hand and together you run into the lake, submerging yourselves, the cells of your body coming alive in the refreshing water.

Breathing in, you and your child sit in the grass, by the lake, looking at a beautiful flower.

Breathing out, you each reach out and lightly touch a delicate petal.

Breathing in, as day turns to night, you and your child lie in the grass and stare up at the beautiful moon.

Breathing out, you observe all the space surrounding the bright moon.

Breathing in, you see a bed, with a white sheet. You are many years older; you have reached the end of your life, and you lie comfortably on the bed.

Breathing out, you feel a warm touch to your hand, and, looking up, you see your child, now many years older. You look into your child's eyes and see the eyes of the child who once crawled into your arms. You see the small child to whom you once taught the difference between right and wrong. You see the child with whom you went on vacations, and from time to time, disagreed. You see the child who grew up to become his or her own beautiful person.

Breathing in, you look to your child and smile.
Breathing out, your child smiles back as a tear runs down your child's cheek.

Breathing in, you reach up with your aged finger to touch the tear.
Breathing out, you feel the wet drop and you release into the unknown. As your eyes close, and all becomes quiet, you feel the warmth of your child's hand embracing your own.

Breathing in, you sense yourself as an ocean, vast and infinite.
Breathing out, your child and your child's children swim and play in your water.

Breathing in, you sense yourself as a mountain.
Breathing out, you see your child climbing. You protect your child with trees that have strong roots and sturdy pathways.

Breathing in, you sense yourself as the moon.
Breathing out, you see your child, now much older than you ever were, staring up at you, smiling. You smile at your child.

Breathing in, you sense yourself as a flower.
Breathing out, you feel a cool breeze blow through your delicate petals, and you know it is your child.

Being

Bring yourself into relaxation with the Calming Exercise found on page 148.

Visualize the moment you first laid eyes on your beautiful child. Look deeply into your child's eyes and smile. You notice your child looking at you, gazing into your eyes. You are everything to your child. . . .

Your child smiles. You smile. . . .

Now imagine yourself lying on your back in a field of green grass. The sky is deep blue, and a gentle wind blows. Hold your baby in your arms and kiss her. Place her in your hands and lift her into the air above your chest. Look at your beautiful child against the blue sky. . . .

Feel the cool breeze flowing around the two of you. . . .

Your child is so light. You feel as though you could let go and your child would remain floating in the air above you. Your baby is so much a part of you. You feel as though you are the same person. And you know that with every passing day, you separate from your child, little by little. . . .

Look up at your baby. Sense the desire deep inside both of you for your child to be close to you. Feel the love driving that desire. And now, sense an opposing tug, gently pulling your child away from you. . . .

Ponder the source of that gentle tug. How does it make you feel? . . .

Now, with an awareness of those opposing forces—bringing your child in and tugging her away from you—slowly relax your fingers from around your child's body and notice that your child floats a few inches from your fingers. . . .

Breathe deeply as you behold your precious child floating in the air. Your child smiles. Thanks you. You are such a wonderful parent.

Feel the presence of your child floating above you. . . .

Exhale deeply and sense your breath reaching your child. Your child feels your breath and inhales it. And as your child exhales, the out-breath slowly flows down to you and you inhale it deep into your lungs. Engage in this exchange for a few breaths.

(pause thirty seconds)

With your eyes still closed, sensing your child's presence above you, you begin to visualize your child growing up. Perhaps your child is very young. Or maybe your child is older. This meditation will now explore your child's life on this Earth. When you reach a point that exceeds your child's age, allow yourself to sense your child beyond that point in time.

Visualize your child taking her first steps. . . .

Can you see your child's smile?

While your child is taking her first steps, bring your awareness back to your child floating above you. . . .

Sense your child's presence. Breathe in your child's out-breath. Your child is always here with you. . . .

Now, imagine your child a little older, blowing out birthday candles. . . .

Count the candles on the cake. You can taste the sweet frosting. . . .

Visualize the stream of air flowing out of your child's mouth to the flames dancing on the candles, the delicate wisps of smoke that rise into the air. Where are those wisps now? Can you sense their presence out in the cosmos? . . .

Imagine your child riding a bicycle, gliding down a pathway, with no resistance. . . .

Observe the pleasure in your child's smile as your eyes meet. Can you see your child in school, playing with other children?

(pause thirty seconds)

And now, turn your attention to the child floating above you, inches from your fingertips. You can feel her presence. Were you to reach out even a little bit, you would touch your child. But you don't. You know your child is there. Your child is always there—always with you. . . .

Breathing slowly and deeply, sense that your child is ready to leave home. Perhaps your child is heading off to college, or is ready to make her own way in the world. You kiss your child good-bye and watch as she walks away. You stand alone in the doorway of your home. Remember how she was once so young, your little baby.

(pause thirty seconds)

Bring your awareness to your beautiful child floating above you. . . .

Time has passed and you witness your child as a parent, playing with her own child. Feel the joy of this moment. The happiness your child feels. You exchange loving glances with your child. . . .

This moment exists because of you. The emotions you feel, you feel because of your connection to your child. Can you sense the nature of your feelings? . . .

Bring your attention to your baby floating above you. With your next inhalation, breathe in your child's soft out-breath. Your child breathes in your out-breath. Slowly, your child moves toward you a few inches, remaining but a hair's width from your hands. . . .

Now, imagine your child at a time and place when you no longer live on this Earth. You have passed on. . . .

Sense your child in motion. Look to your child's face. Your child is filled with joy, living fully on this beautiful planet, Earth. Your child cannot be with you physically anymore. But your child knows you are there, watching. Your child feels your love. . . .

Your child has grown very old. She has had a full and wonderful life. . . .

You can see her, older than you ever were, moving slowing, lying down in bed. As your child's body sinks into the comfortable bed, someone who loves her wraps a blanket around her to keep her warm, and kisses her on the cheek. . . .

Your child smiles and closes her eyes. Your little baby feels deep peace. . . .

Returning awareness to your outstretched hands, you feel your child's body pressing again into your fingers. You open your eyes and see your child, smiling down at you from up in the air. . . .

Your chest aches for your child and you bring her in to you, wrapping your arms around her. You feel your child's body rise as you inhale and sink into you as you exhale. In a few moments, when you exhale again, your child's body will dissolve into a thousand dazzling stars. . . .

Inhale deeply. As you begin your exhalation, you feel your child's body, and then watch as it transforms into the open space as gleaming stars surround you. . . .

Lower your arms as the stars sink into you, your body absorbing them. . . .

Visualize your body as vast open space, filled with galaxies—filled with the love of your child and with your love for your child. One love. . . .

Slowly begin to stir, wiggling your shoulders, fingers, and toes as this meditation comes to an end. Breathe deeply. The image of your newborn baby floating above you is one that may bring you great comfort and a sense of deep connection with your child, throughout your life. Take a moment to reflect on that image and the feelings it evokes. Know that you may return to it anytime. And know that your connection with your child is as deep today as it was the moment you first laid eyes on your beautiful baby.

Meditation on the Vastness of Space in Small Places

The "Driving on the Freeway" verse, found on page 57, asks you to imagine yourself as a blood cell floating within your child's body. The verse also invites you to consider the space surrounding you and to sense its vastness within the body. For many of us, this is difficult because we do not appreciate the expansiveness of space in our lives. The following visualization offers a perspective from which to contemplate just how spacious our world is, both inside and outside.

Find a comfortable place where you can close your eyes and not be distracted for about five minutes. Bring yourself into relaxation with the Calming Exercise found on page 148.

Close your eyes and imagine yourself traveling through outer space. . . .

As you travel in blackness, from time to time you approach and pass stars and planets, filling the space before you with beautiful hues and temperature shifts. . . .

You enter our solar system and arc awed by the size of the heavenly bodies and the vastness of the space between these heavy, seemingly suspended, round objects. . . .

Slowly you pass the planets as you make your way toward Earth, which appears as a small blue marble off in the distance. . . .

As you continue moving through open space, huge planets with orbiting moons slowly recede into the distance. Earth becomes larger, and the black space surrounding it diminishes as oceans and land masses come into focus, followed by snowcapped mountain ranges, canyons, and trees. . . .
(pause thirty seconds)

You begin to see buildings, homes, and people. Then, your child comes into focus and you look into his eyes. . . .

Your child's eyes may be blue as the marble Earth, brown as its rich soil, or green as the trees' leaves. You become smaller and smaller as you enter one of your child's eyes and begin a journey through a blood vessel. . . .

You see nerves, and you float like a blood cell along a capillary, bringing oxygen to your child's brain. It seems that you are as small as you can be. . . .

With your eyes still closed, shift your eyeballs sharply to the right and jump into the subatomic world within your child. There is a penetrating stillness to this space. . . .

You observe huge atoms, surrounded by great distances of space. Small, flickering-blue electrons orbit the proton centers of these heavenly bodies. As you journey on, you find yourself surrounded by a spaciousness as vast as that you found in the far reaches of outer space. . . .

Breathe deeply, knowing you are inside the cosmic expanse of your child's being. . . .

As this visualization draws to a close, ponder the vastness of space—all space. . . .

The distance between our hands can be enormous. As close as we may bring them together, the tiniest gap can take an eternity to cross. We fool ourselves into thinking there is not enough space, not enough time, when there is more than we could ever consume or comprehend.

Child Is the Cosmos

Bring yourself into relaxation with the Calming Exercise found on page 148.

Slowly inhale through your nose, drawing your breath deep into your belly. Exhale through your nose, slowly pushing the air out from your belly. Pause briefly between exhalation and inhalation. Repeat this three times, with each breath lulling you into a deeper state of relaxation. . . .

Close your eyes and visualize your child sitting before you. If your child is an infant, cradle your child in your arms. If your child has not yet been born, carefully cup your tiny baby in the palms of your hands. If your child is sitting in a chair, reach your arms out and hold her hands in your own. Breathe deeply and smile as you make eye contact with your child. . . .

Gaze into your child's eyes and let your sight rest on her small, round pupils. Sense a weightless part of yourself moving toward your child's eyes. You become smaller as you approach your child, and you float into one of her pupils. You feel as though you are in a cave. It is pitch-black. . . .

Imagine the depth of deep space. Sense the vast reach of this emptiness, spreading endlessly in all directions. With your next breath, inhale this open space. . . .

Imagine this energizing space filling not just your lungs but your whole body. Sense your body softening and expanding to create room to accept this space. This silent, open space spreads beyond your body and fills the room or place you are in. Imagine it filling the Earth. . . .

As you exhale, sense the vast emptiness of this silent, open space leaving your body, leaving the room, and leaving the

Earth, as it fills again the far reaches of outer space. Hold your breath for a few seconds as you float amid absolute stillness in the far reaches of deep space. Consider the temperature: Is it cool? Is it warm? . . .

Now, breathing comfortably, visualize a bright pinpoint of white light centered within the heart of the deep, black void of space. Watch the light as it grows larger and begins to pulse. The pulse is familiar to you. It pulses in rhythm with your beating heart. Breathe deeply and concentrate on the rhythm. Slow the rhythm down so that it meets the internal rhythm of your breathing. In and out. In and out.

As you begin to breathe in time with the pulse, you feel yourself moving toward the light. . . .

The light is millions of miles away, yet the journey is effortless. Time is imperceptible, as the bright pinpoint of white light grows larger and brighter. You continue to travel toward the light as it becomes a large, round, brilliantly glowing white orb.

(pause fifteen seconds)

The orb burns bright, but you can safely look directly at it. As you gaze at the white orb, a penetrating blue light appears in its center. Your breathing is steady and slow. . . .

The blue dot slowly grows larger and larger, increasing slightly each time your heart beats. As it grows, you come to see that it has three dimensions. It is a sphere. When it becomes large enough, you reach out and touch it. . . .

As you move your hand around its surface in one direction, it feels cool. As you move your hand around its surface in another, it feels warm.

Soon the blue sphere fills almost all the space.

Look deeply into the blue sphere. Clear your mind. With crisp clarity, you realize that the blue-and-green sphere is the Earth. . . .

Ever so slowly, you begin to move toward the Earth. All it takes is the slightest thought and, effortlessly, your body begins to move. You are still hundreds of thousands of miles away, but coming perceptibly closer with every breath. As you approach the Earth, you reach your hands out toward it. You can envision your hands cupping the Earth. . . .

White clouds are swirling around the Earth's edges, its surface a deep blue and green. Sense your body, its position—your hands floating in front of you. You curl your legs into your belly. You see the water, the land, and the clouds. Relax at the beauty of this scene.

(pause fifteen seconds)

Breathe deeply as an image of your child as a newborn appears before you. . . .

You notice your child's beautiful features, and that your child's eyes are closed, soft lids covering them lightly. Smile as your newborn's eyes open. As you look at her eyes, you see the white clouds surrounding the blue-and-green Earth. . . .

And at the center of the Earth, you see the deep black of empty space. . . .

Look at your beautiful child and gaze gently into her eyes. Smile as you sense her infinite presence, her infinite wisdom, her infinite embrace. . . .

Gaze into your child's eyes. Breathing deeply, look into your child's black pupils and consider the vastness of space. From so small a place, a portal to the cosmos. . . . (Every time you see or visualize your child, your awareness can open to the infinite in your child.)

Expand your awareness to include the white portion of her eyes, and feel the movement of the clouds that continually circle the Earth, producing rain and snow. . . .

Now, bring your awareness to the blue of your newborn's eyes. Breathe deeply and slowly for a few minutes, and contemplate whether the cosmos gave birth first to your child, or to the Earth.

(pause one minute)

Hands and Heart

Bring yourself into relaxation with the Calming Exercise found on page 148.

With eyes open, clench each hand, one at a time. Feel the weight of fingertips pressing against palms. Feel palms pressing against fingertips. To strengthen these sensations, breathe deeply and slowly. On the inhalation, feel fingertips pressing against palms. On the exhalation, feel palms pressing against fingertips. Squeeze as tightly as you can and then relax. You may be able to feel a subtle tingling within your hands.

Now, close your eyes and release your hands so that they rest open by your side. Visualize a red glow emanating from within each hand. . . .

Breathe deeply. Allow each inhalation to bring fresh air to your lungs, and then, when the air reaches the lungs, allow the air to pour into your arms all the way down to the fingertips. . . .

With each breath drawn into your fingers, sense the red glow growing brighter. With each exhalation and release of air, sense the red glow dimming ever so slightly. . . .

Imagine your child sitting across from you and facing you. He is breathing deeply and looking down toward his hands. . . .

Look to your child's hands, resting by their side. Like yours, they are pulsing red. . . .

Are they pulsing at the same rate as yours? Is the red glow as bright as yours? . . .

Perhaps so; perhaps not. Just notice what is at this moment. No need to try to change anything. As your child lifts his eyes to face yours, look at his beautiful face and smile at your child. Your child smiles back at you. . . .

Imagine raising your hands so that they appear before your face. . . .

Look at each finger, the red glow emanating from within. Your child also raises his hands. All four hands are raised and close to each other. . . .

Do you feel the tingle surrounding each hand? Take a few moments to pour your awareness into these hands. They are alive. The tingle, which may be very slight, is that of your hand's awakening—coming to life. . . .

Smile as you welcome your hands back into the experience of life. . . .

Begin to clap your hands—both you and your child, together. Start with a soft clap. Sense the press of tingling palms. Let one or more claps fill the space within each deep breath. Gradually, increase the rate of clapping. . . .

Smile as you and your child clap together in unison. For the next minute, sense yourself clapping with your child.
(pause one minute)

Visualize the red glow moving back and forth with the motion of the hands, sense the tingling of the hands, and allow breaths of air to pour deep into the lungs, filling the belly, and then out along the arms to feed the fingertips. . . .

During the next several moments, enjoy the pleasure of looking at your child's beautiful smile. This is a joyful time. . . .

Notice how the clapping sound fills the silence with a beautiful rhythm. It is the rhythm of you and your child. Feel free to clap as loudly and rapidly or as softly and slowly as you like. Feel free to mix it up. It doesn't matter who sets the pace. Lead and let your child lead. Let it happen without intention.

(pause for three minutes)

While continuing to clap, visualize the red glow, feel the tingle, and share smiles. Notice how the rate of clapping approximates a heartbeat. If you sense the clapping is faster than your heartbeat, then slow your clapping. If you sense the clapping is slower than your heartbeat, then clap a little faster. Bring the tempo of clapping in line with the tempo of your heartbeat.

(pause for a minute)

As this visualization comes to a close, slowly raise your arms that have patiently been sitting by your side, and begin to clap as you continue to hear the clapping sound produced by your imagined hands. Slowly, open your eyes and look at your hands. Smile.

Cleansing the Earth

Bring yourself into relaxation with the Calming Exercise found on page 148.

Close your eyes. When your eyelids touch, smile, knowing that you are giving yourself this moment of deep relaxation, and that you will begin to feel a deeper connection with your child. Smile as you inhale. Smile as you exhale. . . .

Direct your awareness to your hands. If they are touching, separate them, placing one on each side of your body in a comfortable place. Breathe air into your body and imagine the air filling your lungs and then moving out to your arms and flowing down to your hands. . . .

As the air reaches the ends of your fingers, feel it bounce against the inside of your fingertips. Each time you inhale and the air bounces against your fingertips, visualize blue sparks leaping off of your nails. . . .

Take a few moments to breathe in and out slowly. With every inhalation, let the air lightly bounce, always the same light bounce, against the inside of your fingertips. . . .

As you sink into greater relaxation, let the blue sparks grow larger and more vibrant. Your fingers and hand may begin to tingle. That's okay. Your fingers and hands are waking up. . . .

Imagine your hands slowly stretching out before you. . . .

Visualize them if you can. If that is difficult, then sense that they are there in front of you, a linen cloth draped over them.

As you continue to breathe, imagine squeezing your hands open and shut several times. . . .

Squeeze them as you exhale, forcing the air out of your lungs and outside of your body. Open them as you inhale, with the rush of air filling your lungs and pouring into your hands. Blue sparks leap out from your fingers as the air lightly caresses each fingertip. . . .

Now, sense your child's hands placed on top of yours. . . .

You can feel your child's palms resting on top of your hands. They are soft; the feeling is subtle. You want to turn your hands over and hold his hand, but you don't. Just breathe in and out as you sense your child's hands. . . .

At first, blue sparks leave only your fingers and not your child's. But soon, you sense blue sparks leaving his fingers as well. . . .

The blue sparks are now being emitted from both your fingers and your child's fingers, in synchronization. . . .

Now, imagine your child sitting across from you, hands outstretched. Your fingertips are a few inches apart. Your hands are tingling, and you feel an even greater tingling sensation each time the blue sparks emitted from your child's fingers touch yours. . . .

At the same time, your blue sparks are touching your child's fingers. Look into his face and see him smiling at you. Smile back. . . .

Lean forward and wrap your arms around your child. As your hands settle firmly against his back, release the blue sparks into him, energizing your child's body. . . .

At the same time, feel your child's arms, embracing you, releasing a surge of blue sparks into your body. The sparks course up and down your spine, filling your heart and other organs with your child's health-filled energy. . . .

Feel the sparks move into your brain, clearing away any clutter and baggage that you've been wanting to release. . . .

Slowly, when you are ready, release your embrace and imagine yourself returning to an upright position. . . .

Breathe in and out slowly, and imagine you and your child smiling at each other. . . .

Now, sense yourself rubbing your hands together. Do this slowly at first. Feel each hand as it rubs against the other. . . .

Notice whether your palms are coarse or soft. Feel the tingling. As you do this, your hands begin to glow a deep red, and you can sense the glow from within their core. You feel the warmth. . . .

As you continue to rub your hands together, the red glows brighter, and soon you see and feel orange sparks emanating from them. . . .

As you are doing this, you see that your child is doing the same. You notice his hands glowing red from within and you see bright orange sparks leaving his hands. . . .

Observe the many bright little orange sparks surrounding your hands and your child's hands. The sparks resemble small lightning bolts. . . .

As you visualize or sense you and your child sitting opposite one another, rubbing hands, and you see the orange sparks continually emitted from your hands, begin to pull away from this image and see the black space that surrounds and flows between you and your child. . . .

As this black space surrounding you continues to grow, and you see farther and farther beyond the two of you, you sense a rubbery membrane at the outer edge of this space. . . .

You cannot move much more than the rubbing motion of your hands, and you begin to lean forward, bringing your head and upper torso into contact with your legs. . . .

You see yourself in this crouched position, sitting alongside your child. Your hands are pressed close to your chests, as the glowing red of your hands soaks into your chests and your hearts begin to glow red and pulse. . . .

You breathe in and out slowly to the rhythm of your beating hearts.

(pause one minute)

Now, your focus returns to you and your child as the surrounding black space moves away from the membrane. . . .

You come to see only you and your child and black space. You now see that the black space spreads out endlessly in all directions. . . .

As with each inhalation, you see a point of bright white light filling the black space off in the distance. There are now two—and now, three points of light. They begin to flicker as more and more points of light begin to fill the space all around you. Before you know it, there are points of light all around you, and you sense that they spread outward, endlessly, in every direction. . . .

You now focus your attention on the black space between you and your child. . . .

You and your child are now each rubbing your hands together as a red glow fills the space where your hands almost touch. Orange sparks surround your fingers and hands. . . .

You see a small blue point of light floating between you and your child. You shift your perspective as you begin to move closer and closer to the blue point, which is growing into a small orb. . . .

You continue to feel your hands rubbing together, tingling. . . .

The blue orb grows larger and larger, and you see emerging in this blue sphere, patches of green, and an outer swirl of white.

As you move closer and closer to the blue orb, you feel the orange sparks flying off in every direction around you. You can sense soft pinpricks against your face wherever the orange sparks bounce off your face. It does not hurt. As the sparks touch you, you feel energized. . . .

Then, you feel yourself enter a large white cloud that is damp and cool as you continue to approach the blue-and-green sphere. You feel yourself traveling through the center of this cloud and then moving out the other side. As you emerge from the white puff, you see the Earth far below you. Lightning fills the atmosphere and, for the first time, you begin to hear the crack and rumble of thunder from far away. It is a continuous sound. . . .

The lightning cleanses the atmosphere as it transforms oxygen into ozone, and you begin to smell the fresh scent of the outdoors after a thunderstorm. . . .

With every inhalation, you bring fresh air into your body. The fresh air fills the atmosphere. You observe the blue-and-green Earth becoming more and more pristine with every breath you take. . . .

Slowly, you recede from this close-up view of the Earth. You travel back through the clouds as the Earth becomes smaller and smaller, until it returns to a tiny blue point of light between you and your child. . . .

You look up and see your child smiling at you. You smile back. . . .

Slowly, you stop rubbing you hands together and reach out to touch your child's hands. Perhaps you feel a tiny shock or tingle when your hands touch.

Breathing deeply and slowly, open your eyes. . . .

Take a few moments to absorb the sensations of the meditation.

Closing

As human beings, we open ourselves to a tremendous bounty of joy when we establish and maintain connections to other human beings, to animals, and to all nature. In particular, our connection to our children is deeply rooted in our being, and the significant physical and emotional presence of our children in our lives serves to make that connection especially consequential. We naturally feel boundless love and affection for our children, but the routine of our day-to-day existence can cause us to lose track not only of the enormity of these feelings, but also of the presence of our children in our lives. As a result, the full measure of joy and affection that flows from our connection with our children becomes compromised. Mindful parenting helps us maintain our awareness of our child. By so doing, the connection between us and our child becomes robust, marked by an easy, natural, and continuous flow of energy, emotion, and compassion that serves to enhance feelings of joyfulness and bliss in our everyday lives.

Mindfulness can center on the breath, on our immediate physical environment, on persons and animals, and can extend out to the whole of the cosmos. We can be mindful of things close at hand, and things at the other end of the universe. Ultimately, there is no difference, because our breathing and the undulating energy of the cosmos are the same, and everything in between is connected to our breathing and to the cosmos. Mindful parenting entails the conscious decision to pay specific attention to a special part of the world around us—our children. More than anything else, our relationship with our children can lend itself to a powerful and more natural mindfulness practice.

Appendices

Appendix A

Twelve-Step Mind-Body Flow Exercise

The Twelve-Step Mind-Body Flow Exercise will help you to transform routine moments into mindful moments of awakening. As this process takes root, the light of mindful awareness will shine brighter, longer, and more often. As is elaborated below, this exercise forms the heart of the following pathway of awakening:

You bring attention to a part of your child's body

You redirect attention to that part of your own body

You begin the exercise starting with that part of your body

The exercise brings you more deeply into your body, opening awareness to the present moment

After you review and rehearse the exercise set forth on the next page, you will find it easy to implement. The difficult part is remembering to implement it. This is where the practice of mindful parenting comes into play. The verses and meditations contained in this book will help you to more naturally and spontaneously open awareness to the presence of your child in your life. Each time this happens, you have the opportunity to expand awareness to the present moment. To do this, let your awareness of your child, if not already directed to a part of the body (e.g., heart, hands, smile, eyes) rest on a part of your child's body. Then, bring your attention to that same part of your body. From there, you initiate the Twelve-Step Mind-Body Flow Exercise.

Exercise Instructions

Take a few moments and rehearse this exercise. Use your hands where indicated, as they serve as markers to help make the exercise more energetic and memorable. You should find this flow intuitive and easy to engage. The more time you spend committing it to memory, the more frequently you will find yourself applying it during your day.

1. While sitting or standing, rest your hands on the crown of your head. Feel the bottoms of your palms pressing against the top of your skull. Inhale. As you breathe, direct your awareness to the tiny space between your hands and head.

2. Slowly lift your hands and lower them to your side. As you do, keep your awareness concentrated on the top of your head, to the space where your hands rested.

3. Then, allow awareness to spread around your whole head. Rotate your eyeballs and feel them inside their sockets. Wrinkle your nose. Smile and lick your lips. Feel the wetness of your tongue. Touch your chin lightly with one of your hands. Continue to breathe.

4. Turn your head from side to side and sense the muscles supporting your neck. If you like, lift and then wrap your hands gently around the back of your neck for support, or to better control the motion.

5. Lightly twist your shoulders back and forth and relax your arms. Wriggle your fingers, exhaling, as you direct awareness to them.

6. Gently expand your chest, creating space within your body cavity, and lower your shoulder blades.

7. Touch one of your hands to your belly and take a deep, full breath. Sense your hand expanding with your belly. Feel the empty hollow and stillness within your expanding stomach. (This is felt most fully on an empty stomach.)

8. Gently shake or move your legs and bring awareness to your knees.

9. Lift yourself slightly onto the balls of your feet, feeling your weight pressing against your toes.

10. Relax onto your heels and feel the bottoms of your feet pressing firmly against the ground. Breathe as you ground yourself, feeling solid and stable against the Earth. With your feet firmly planted on the ground, remind yourself that you are alive and present on this Earth.

11. As you awaken to this realization, bring your awareness upward to your chest and take a full breath, breathing in through your nose.

12. On your next inhalation, bring your awareness upward to the top of your head. Look up at the sky and observe the colors. Is there a breeze? Take a moment and consider what you see around you and how you are feeling. Smile.

When you complete this exercise, you will find yourself in a very different place from where you were when you began it, only a few moments earlier. You are alert. The brief body scan moves aliveness into your body, redirecting energy that had been caught up feeding your thoughts. At the end, as you shift attention up from your feet to your lungs to your eyes, you activate your body in a way that is ideal for mindful awareness. Your feet ground you. Your breathe frees you. Your awareness expands.

Appendix B

Breathing Exercise

Many of the verses and meditations explicitly invite you to breathe deeply during the mindful experience. This is because so many of us are typically shallow breathers, or our breathing becomes shallow as we become excited or agitated, regardless of whether we label it desirable or undesirable. We owe it to ourselves to breathe more fully. In doing so, we bring a needed dose of healthfulness into our lives. For example, we have more energy, our posture improves, and we gently massage our internal organs. The mindful verses and meditations present ideal opportunities to engage deliberately in more healthful breathing. If thinking about your breathing is new to you, consider incorporating some of the suggestions listed below.

1. Relax your body as you prepare to inhale: Drop your shoulders, relax your jaw, release your tongue from the roof of your mouth, uncross your arms and legs, spread your fingers and toes open, and soften your gaze.

2. Slowly draw in your breath, expanding your belly.

3. Visualize the air entering your nostrils (preferably) or mouth and making its way into your lungs.

4. Feel your belly expand, followed by your chest expanding.

5. Pause with the breath deep within your body.

6. Slowly release the air through your nostrils or mouth.

7. Visualize the air as it flows out of your body.

Appendix C

Mindful Parent Children's Story

One Day Winston the Wave Woke Up

The practice of mindful parenting takes on a special character when you are with your child. Beauty and grace arise spontaneously when you are able to be present and listen deeply. While all interactions share this potential, it is not always realized. The story of *Winston the Wave* is one that encourages mindful awareness. Read it with your child and explore its messages together.

One Day Winston the Wave Woke Up

Winston looked up and saw the golden sun. He smiled as puffs of clouds glided across the deep blue sky. Winston had always known the sun, sky, and clouds.

Winston stretched and took a deep breath. He felt the warmth of the sun deep inside of him. Winston looked around and saw a forever filled with blue and green water. The ocean flowed out endlessly, as it always did.

Winston closed his eyes and dipped down into the ocean. All at once, Winston felt himself as large as the ocean. Winston poked his head up out of the ocean and smiled.

Appendix C

Winston looked down, deep into the ocean, and saw beautiful fish, squeezy sponges, colorful coral, and dancing seaweed, all floating together in sweet harmony.

Winston closed his eyes again and felt the fish swim through him. Winston felt himself pour through the tiny little holes in the sponges. The coral swayed this way and that, and Winston swayed with it. Winston bobbed up and down with the seaweed.

As Winston danced, turning in all directions, he saw something in the distance that he had never seen before. What could it be?

For the first time ever, Winston wondered.

Off in the distance, Winston saw a small white speck. Perhaps it was a bird, thought Winston. But the speck did not fly away. As Winston watched the speck, he saw it grow larger and larger. It was not a bird.

And for the first time ever, Winston realized he did not know something.

As the speck continued to grow, Winston realized that the blue-green ocean was not the only thing surrounding him. Off in the distance, instead of nothing but endless ocean, Winston saw a thin white line stretching across the horizon. Winston did not know what it was.

And for the first time ever, Winston felt confused.

The thin white line continued to grow larger, and Winston saw that it was white sand. Winston had only seen sand on the bottom of the ocean. But there it was. Winston did not understand why it was there.

Winston sank into the ocean depths and became the ocean. He breathed in and out, and became the wind. Winston poked his head up again and smiled. He felt protected and safe. But when he turned around, he saw the white sand again. This time it was even closer to him than before.

And for the first time ever, Winston worried.

Winston did not want to get any closer to the white sand. He tried to stay where he was, but it was no use. As hard as he tried, the white sand slowly but surely kept coming closer.

And for the first time ever, Winston felt frustrated.

Winston stared at the white sand as it moved closer and closer. Winston wondered what it meant for there to be sand way up as high as the top of the ocean. And he wondered what would happen to him if he got too close to the sand.

And for the first time ever, Winston felt scared.

While worrying, Winston forgot all about the beautiful blue sky and sun. He forgot about the clouds, the wind, and the ocean. Winston forgot that there were fish and sponges and coral and seaweed. Winston could think of only one thing—the white sand, which kept coming closer and kept getting bigger.

Because it was worrying him so, Winston thought of what he could do. Winston decided he would try not to think of the white sand.

Winston instead tried to become as large as the ocean—but all he could do was look at the ocean. He tried to fly with the wind—but all he could do was think of the wind blowing by. He tried to flow with the sea creatures—but all he could do was see how pretty they were.

And for the first time ever, Winston felt alone

Winston began to wonder whether the sand was still there, and what would happen to all of the beautiful things around him if the sand got too close to him.

And for the first time ever, Winston felt sad.

Winston did not want to feel alone. He smiled as he remembered the ocean, and the feel of the wind, and how pretty the sea creatures were. And for a little while, Winston was happy.

Then Winston remembered the sand and he stopped feeling happy. He stopped breathing, too, for a little while. Slowly,

Winston looked around to where the white sand was. It was still there. It was still getting closer.

And for the first time ever, Winston did not know what to do.

So Winston did nothing. He closed his eyes. He sat very still and slowly breathed in and out. He breathed in and out and in and out. He did this for a long time. The white sand was very close now, and Winston could feel himself being pulled toward it. The pull was becoming stronger and stronger. Winston did not resist the pull.

Without thinking about what to do, Winston closed his eyes and sank into the ocean. He felt the flow of all the creatures in the ocean, just as he had before. Winston took a deep breath and began to rock with the sound of the wind and the flow of the coral and the seaweed.

As he exhaled, he felt himself become as big as the ocean and as wide-open as the sky. He began to fly with the wind. He flowed through all the sea creatures, and in and out of the sea sponges.

Then Winston saw white sand coming up all around him. Winston was so close that he heard the sound of the ocean and the wind breaking against the sand. It was a sound he had never heard before.

Appendix C

But as Winston flew with the wind—as open as the sky and as deep as the ocean—and as Winston flowed with the coral and the sea creatures, he recognized the sound from somewhere, from a time long ago.

It was a sound that was deep inside of him. It was a sound that he'd known all his life. Winston listened to the sound deep inside of him, and he understood that he was not alone.

Winston was the ocean.
Winston was the sky.
Winston was the sun.
Winston was the wind.
Winston was the fish and the coral and the sponges and the seaweed.
Winston was the sand.

Winston realized that he was so much more than any one thing. And Winston was no longer worried or confused. He was not scared or frustrated. And Winston no longer felt alone or sad.

And as Winston felt himself roll out of the ocean and onto the white sand, he felt himself sink deep into the cool, moist Earth.

And Winston smiled.

The End . . . And Then Again

Learn More about Mindful Parenting

To learn more about mindful parenting, visit The Mindful Parent® website at:

www.themindfulparent.org

In addition to providing information on mindful parenting, the website publishes verses submitted by parents and child-care givers from around the world. If reading this book inspires you to create a mindful-parenting verse, consider submitting it to The Mindful Parent®. A submission form is linked to from the website's home page. You can contact us directly by sending an e-mail to info@themindfulparent.org.

The Mindful Parent® publishes and podcasts *The Morning Cup*, a daily column that presents mindful-parenting tips and verses. You can read *The Morning Cup* on the website and listen to it and other mindful-parenting recordings on The Mindful Parent® Podcast, found at:

www.themindfulparent.org/podcast/

If you would like to receive information about mindful-parenting workshops, and special events, send an e-mail to us at: events@themindfulparent.org.

We look forward to hearing from you and learning of your mindful-parenting insights and experiences.

About the Cover

The cover image is of an argillite stone carving by Canadian Inuit artist, John Tiktak (1916-1981), who was drawn to the emotional theme of mother and child. As noted by Robert Kardosh, curator of the Marion Scott Gallery in Vancouver, British Columbia,

> In these serene works the child often emerges organically from the mother's back, as though an extension of the latter, expressing in simple and moving terms the maternal bond that is fundamental in Inuit culture.

I am grateful to my mother, Susan Rogers, for her gift of this remarkable piece. It is a fitting image to adorn the cover of this book as it effortlessly transmits the grace and power of mindful parenting. As in all of the "mother and child" representations found in the work of Tiktak, the parent is present and stable—what could be more present than being fixed in earthen stone? It should come as no surprise, then, that the child is present, content, and joyful.

About the Author

Scott Rogers received his master's degree in social psychology and his law degree from the University of Florida in Gainesville. He has enjoyed a lifelong interest in mindfulness and the ways in which the mind and body move toward and retreat from present-moment awareness. In 1991 he began his formal training in meditation, and now works with people interested in learning how to meditate and become more mindful. Rogers is one of the leaders of the Miami Beach Sangha, a mindfulness-based meditation group.

In 2003 Rogers founded the online mindful-parenting community, The Mindful Parent, which is located on the Internet at www.themindfulparent.org, and publishes *The Morning Cup*, a daily column and podcast containing mindful-parenting tips. The website also publishes verses contributed by parents and child-care givers from around the world. In 2005 he produced *Child Is the Cosmos*, a CD containing mindful-parenting meditations and visualizations, and he is currently working on a second CD, *An Introduction to the Joys of Mindful Parenting*, to be released in the summer of 2006. Rogers lives in Miami Beach, Florida, with his wife, Pam, and two daughters, Millie and Rose.

About the Artist

Jorge Perez-Rubio was born in the United States in 1969 to Cuban parents. He was raised in the Caribbean, Europe, and the United States, and after graduating from Sarah Lawrence College with a major in philosophy and fine arts, he settled in

New York City. Perez-Rubio worked as an artist and art teacher, continuing his studies at The School of Visual Arts, The Art Students League of New York, and the National Academy School of Fine Arts.

From 2000 to 2003 he lived and taught in Cairo, Egypt. This experience added to his Latin heritage a strong cultural tie to North Africa and the Middle East. Perez-Rubio has continued to develop his style while studying calligraphy and ancient writing. He is a master draftsman, and believes that art in education builds bridges between people and cultures. He firmly believes in the universal appeal of the image, and has a profound appreciation for the common experiences that all people share.

He lives in Miami Beach with his wife, Christine, where he continues to explore his roots and their relationship to his art.

Breinigsville, PA USA
01 December 2010
250437BV00001B/276/A